VGM Opportunities Series

DISCARDED

OPPORTUNITIES IN
LAW ENFORCEMENT
AND CRIMINAL JUSTICE
CAREERS

James D. Stinchcomb

Foreword by
Wesley A. Pomeroy, J.D.
Chief of Police (retired)
Berkeley, California

VGM Career Horizons
a division of *NTC Publishing Group*
Lincolnwood, Illinois USA

T 363. 2023
sti

Cover Photo Credits
Upper right and upper left courtesy of the Chicago Police Department; lower right courtesy of the San Francisco Police Department; lower left courtesy of the U.S. Department of Justice, Federal Bureau of Investigation.

Library of Congress Cataloging-in-Publication Data
Stinchcomb, James D.
    Opportunities in law enforcement and criminal justice careers / James D. Stinchcomb — [Rev. ed]
        p. cm. — (VGM opportunities series)
    Includes bibliographical references.
    ISBN 0-8442-4608-5 (hardcover). — ISBN 0-8442-4609-3 (paperback).
        1. Police—Vocational guidance—United States.   2. Law enforcement—Vocational guidance—United States.   3. Criminal justice, Administration of—Vocational guidance—United States.
    I. Title.   II. Series.
    HV8143.S86   1996
    363.2'023'73—dc20   96-418
                                                              CIP

Davidson   10/96   14.95

Published by VGM Career Horizons, a division of NTC Publishing Group
4255 West Touhy Avenue
Lincolnwood (Chicago), Illinois 60646-1975, U.S.A.

67890VP987654321

CONTENTS

Origin and growth in America. Current outlook. Policing in America
in the 1990s and beyond. Personnel needs. Future outlook.

Personal requirements. Selection requirements. Probation, tenure,
and promotion. The patrol officer. The traffic officer. The detective
or criminal investigator. County units and sheriff's departments.

State police and highway patrol. Civilian positions. Other
regulatory units.

Military. Federal agencies. Typical assignments. For more
information.

Fringe benefits. Other incentives. Frustrations. The element of
danger.

High school. College. Cadet program—a work study plan. Recruit
training. Career development and in-service training.

ABOUT THE AUTHOR

James D. Stinchcomb is presently the Director of the School of Justice and Safety Administration, the regional training center for all of Dade County (Miami) Florida. He was previously an associate professor in and chairman of the Department of Administration of Justice and Public Safety at Virginia Commonwealth University. He has served in Washington, D.C. as the criminal justice staff director for a national consulting firm and previous to that held a full-time consultant assignment with the U.S. Department of Justice under the Law Enforcement Assistance Administration's Law Enforcement Education Program (LEEP).

Previously the author served on the staff of the American Association of Community and Junior Colleges (AACJC) under a Kellogg Foundation grant as specialist for public service education. He was training and education consultant for the International Association of Chiefs of Police under a Ford Foundation grant. He chaired the Department of Police Administration at St. Petersburg (Florida) Junior College and developed the bachelor's degree program in law enforcement offered at Florida State University.

After completing a Bachelor of Science degree in psychology, Director Stinchcomb served in the Louisville, Kentucky, Police Department. He holds a Master of Arts degree in criminology and completed all coursework in the criminology doctoral program at Florida State University. He was a lecturer in the Administration of Justice Program at the University of Pittsburgh and has served as a part-time faculty member at eight other community colleges and universities.

In his consulting capacity, the author has visited more than 150 educational institutions to review and assess their efforts in law enforcement and criminal justice. He was the co-author of two AACJC publications—*Guidelines for Law Enforcement Education Programs in Community and Junior Colleges* and *Law Enforcement Training and the Community College.* In addition he is volume editor of the J. G. Ferguson Publishing Company's *Career Opportunities: Community Service and Related Specialists* and is series editor for all Prentice-Hall criminal justice publications, including both textbooks and training manuals.

In prior years Director Stinchcomb also has served as consultant to the President's Crime Commission on Law Enforcement, the National Sheriffs' Association, Westinghouse Justice Institute, Public Administration Service, and a number of state and local organizations. He was an original member of the grant review panel for the Law Enforcement Education Program under LEAA and served as project director for a U.S. Office of Education grant to develop a curriculum guide for law enforcement programs. His major consultant role was as criminal justice education specialist to the National Planning Association in Washington, D.C. He also serves regularly as an accreditation team member for the American Council on Education in its program to evaluate law enforcement training within the military. Director Stinchcomb is the author of several articles and chapters in college textbooks on police issues.

Most recently he has prepared training evaluation studies for departments from Chicago to St. Petersburg, Florida, and has been called upon to testify regarding proper police training methods.

Director Stinchcomb has an extensive background in managing grant funded activities, some of which include Saudi Arabian Police Training, Computer Based Training Lab development, Juvenile Justice Use of Force curriculum, and a statewide study of the Test for Adult Basic Education for Criminal Justice personnel. He also has assisted local and state governments in writing and preparing grant applications.

FOREWORD

Whether our unique Constitutionally based American democracy continues to flourish or wither depends on how our criminal justice employees carry out their duties and responsibilities. They are among the most important people in society today. Legislators can enact laws, courts can interpret them, agency directors can establish policy, politicians can attempt to influence policy, and the public can pass judgment, but it is the police officer—on the street seven days a week, twenty-four hours a day, who must make on-the-spot decisions while dealing with problems and critical issues—who truly reflects the values and ethics of our society.

A law enforcement career is an exciting challenge and a deeply rewarding experience for the men and women who choose it. They must be prepared to act quickly and decisively, but with judicious constraint and compassion. They must always protect the integrity of the rule of law and never act contrary to or outside of the law. They must be prepared, upon occasion, to resist the urging of a frightened or angry public to act unlawfully in stressful times because a perceived danger is said to "justify the means."

A true professional in the criminal justice system knows that the U.S. Constitution and its amendments are the foundation upon which our nation was built. The ideals, rights, and protections expressed therein are the reasons we rebelled against the British rule and established a democratic government. It is important for a police officer to understand that and to act on it, because he or she is the only one in our society who can protect and enforce those rights in any practical way. Knowing that and accepting that responsibility puts into context and makes more coherent the rest of the police officer's responsibilities to enforce statutory and criminal laws and to perform the wide range of other activities required of him or her.

If you decide to join the criminal justice system, you will find that crime fighting is much more than just law enforcement, and corrections is much more than just "guarding." As a matter of fact, most of your time will be spent responding to basic human needs. You will mediate disputes, resolve conflicts, counsel both young and old, assist those most in need, and if you are truly successful, will be looked to for advice and guidance by those you serve.

Law enforcement and corrections are richly rewarding careers. They were when I first entered this field more than fifty years ago, and they still are today! Every aspect of my career—highway patrol, sheriff's department (including corrections), municipal police department, state university security, U.S. Department of Justice, the White House, and now county ombudsman—has been different, but each involved the basic, human interaction that is the core of professional law enforcement.

Director Stinchcomb's *Opportunities in Law Enforcement and Criminal Justice Careers* is an excellent source of information for those who are interested in following a career in law enforcement, corrections, or other related fields. It provides a wealth of valuable, easily understood information that is both useful and practical. If you are one of those interested, you will benefit greatly from this book.

If you really want to make a difference and feel a sense of personal accomplishment, become a police or correctional officer and share our pride and camaraderie. Our nation needs idealistic men and women to serve in this critically important human endeavor.

Wesley A. Pomeroy, J.D.
Chief of Police (retired)
Berkeley, California

ACKNOWLEDGMENT

The author gratefully acknowledges Dr. Jeanne B. Stinchcomb, co-author of the Fox and Stinchcomb, *Introduction to Corrections,* fourth edition (Prentice-Hall), for preparing portions of this manuscript.

CHAPTER 1

OVERVIEW OF LAW ENFORCEMENT AND CRIMINAL JUSTICE

When one views the history of the American police establishment, it is clear that this complex system emerged from circumstances very different from today's mobile and industrialized urban communities. Originally the English system encouraged mutual responsibility and even was known as the *mutual pledge system.* The term "hue and cry" became a familiar one as citizens were alerted to their personal responsibility for preservation of the peace. As time went on, the family grouping known as the "hundred" arose, and out of that era came the constable, whose primary duties related to custody of horses and weapons. Then several *hundreds* merged themselves into *shires,* forming the office of Shire-Reeve. This office, appointed by the crown to keep peace and order, is the source of our modern term "sheriff."

In 1066, William the Conqueror invaded England. Most historians refer to this period as a critical one in legal developments. The philosophy of an enforcement unit separated from the judiciary evolved during this time.

By the late 1200s, England had created a "watch and ward" system for fire protection, guarding the town gate, and nighttime security. Gradually, the constable gained acceptance, and for centuries he was to serve as "conservator" under the justice of the peace.

Gradually, the concept of assigning landowners the responsibility of keeping the king's law gave way to taxation for the purpose of paying men who served as enforcers. In 1777, under King George III, wages were established from taxes, relieving merchants and landowners of the financial burden of law enforcement. Also, by this time, law enforcement had become a demanding task because of the pressures of the

Industrial Revolution. The rural-to-urban migration that accompanied the revolution and the mob violence that led to use of military force paved the way for legislation clearly identifying the civil police.

Many law enforcement experiments before 1820 failed because no system could reconcile individual freedom of action with security of person and property. It remained for Sir Robert Peel, England's Home Secretary, in 1829 to introduce into Parliament the Act for Improving the Police In and Near the Metropolis. This led to the first organized British metropolitan police force, structured along military lines and numbering 1,000 men. These *bobbies*, despite low pay, recruitment problems, and resistance from Parliament, proved so effective that similar units were established throughout England, and by 1856 Parliament had provided for every borough and county to have a police force.

The Peelian Act of 150 years ago set forth principles that are still pertinent today, and they are set down here because they remain as basic tenets of the law enforcement profession:

- The police must be stable, efficient, and organized along military lines.
- The police must be under governmental control.
- The absence of crime will best prove the efficiency of police.
- The distribution of crime news is essential.
- The deployment of police strength, both by time and area, is essential.
- No quality is more indispensable to a police officer than a perfect command of temper; a quiet, determined manner has more effect than violent action.
- Good appearance commands respect.
- The securing and training of proper persons is at the root of efficiency.
- Public security demands that every police officer must be given a number.
- Police headquarters should be centrally located and easily accessible.
- Police should be hired on a probationary basis.
- Police records are necessary for the correct distribution of police strength.

ORIGIN AND GROWTH IN AMERICA

American colonists in the seventeenth and eighteenth centuries brought to America the law enforcement structure with which they were familiar in England. The transfer of the offices of constable and sheriff to rural American areas—which included most colonial territory—was accomplished with little change in the structure of the offices.

Generally speaking, the constable became responsible for law enforcement in the towns, while the sheriff took responsibility for the counties. Also, many colonial cities adopted the nightwatch system; Boston, as early as 1636, had nightwatchmen. The New York nightwatchmen were known as the *rattlewatch* because they carried rattles on their rounds. Gradually, as in England, American cities began to develop their own police forces. Although Philadelphia established such a force in 1833, the ordinance was repealed several years later. In 1838 Boston created a day force to reinforce its nightwatch. In 1844 the New York legislature passed a law creating the first twenty-four-hour organization, and following that model, most major cities unified their day and night forces until by 1870, all cities had full-time police departments. During the remainder of the nineteenth century, a number of efforts were made to reform and improve policing both in the city and in the rural areas. Civil service enactment proved helpful, and some forces moved gradually to merit employment and less political interference. Police training schools emerged in the early 1900s, and, although quite modest, they set a standard that by the mid-twentieth century had become generally accepted.

During the 1920s came the prophetic leadership of Chief August Vollmer at Berkeley; he advertised in the University of California's student newspaper for young men to serve on the police department while obtaining their college education. Vollmer's criteria for selection were simple and direct: "high intelligence, sound nerves, good physique, sterling character, fast reaction time, good memory, and the ability to make accurate observations and correct decisions."

CURRENT OUTLOOK

In 1965 the International Association of Chiefs of Police Advisory Council on Police Education and Training, a group of national authorities assembled under a Ford Foundation Grant, stated that:

...generally, it is conceded that today's law enforcement officer has a need for higher education. It is also generally agreed that within the next few years, law enforcement officers will find higher education imperative. The above observation is the result of consideration of the changes that society has and is experiencing in such areas as the population explosion, the growing pressure for education beyond high school, the changing nature of metropolitan areas, and the effects of tensions and pressures ranging from automation to race. The law enforcement officer is required to meet all kinds of people and innumerable kinds of situations; he or she must therefore:

1. Be equipped to make good value judgements.
2. Be able to maintain one's perspective.
3. Be able to understand underlying causes of human behavior.
4. Be able to communicate clearly and precisely.
5. Possess leadership qualities and make decisions.
6. Be knowledgeable of job skills.

In view of changing conditions which require flexibility, basic theory, and broad understandings, it is concluded that a wide spectrum of higher education must be available.

A published committee report from the International Association of Police Professors (now the Academy of Criminal Justice Sciences) that same year reads as follows:

The transformation of the United States from a rural to an urban society, the tremendous social problems resulting from herding people together in vast conglomerations around urban centers, the rapid acceleration of the drive for equality, the breakdown of many of our institutions which have heretofore maintained social stability, pose problems for police which are greater in both magnitude and complexity than those which they have faced before. We believe they demand changes in some of our approaches to police work. They require an increasing knowledge of the social sciences, especially psychology and sociology, and they require the capacity to adapt an array of technological devices to police work. Furthermore, it seems that at least the larger police departments of this country will not be able to escape the trend toward increasing specialization which is characteristic of virtually all other occupations in American society. This means that law enforcement education programs must be planned so that they will include a core of work in the law enforcement field for all law enforcement officers, plus the opportunity to develop special skills within this broad field.

The federal publication of the National Advisory Commission on Criminal Justice Standards and Goals (1973) again emphasized that college studies were essential to achieving professionalism. It specifically recommended that all police officers have an undergraduate degree no later than 1982. In the meantime, the standards proposed that all police officers should have at least two years of college then, and three years of college by the end of the 1980s.

Although these optimistic timetables were not met universally, in many areas of the nation it is common to find police academies where a majority of recruits possess at least two years of college. Even for departments that may not require college standards, the labor pool is such that applicants possess them.

POLICING IN AMERICA IN THE 1990s AND BEYOND

Legal and procedural complexities have increased so greatly that police officers are expected to have significant knowledge of court decisions regarding searches and seizures, inquiries, and arrests, along with the difficult burden of having to make those decisions on the spot without benefit of analysis and discussion. Officers must also recognize and understand a body of professional knowledge that has emerged from sociology and psychology, but which is more appropriately referred to as human relations, crisis intervention, and crisis management.

Officers also note an increased need to become better generalists on a number of matters relating to safety and crime prevention that previously had not been demanded of all police officers.

In addition technology has become more widespread and will have more impact upon policing than ever was imagined a few decades ago. This will result in the use of more scientific techniques to plot incidents and occurrences, to examine evidence, to collect and assess data, and to aid in predicting events. Although instrumentation, computers, and other technical devices may influence results, street officers will increasingly need to control and manage these devices, as well as interpret their outputs for effective action.

The hard issues of years gone by, such as the role of police officers as crime fighters versus their role as community service agents, may not yet be resolved; however, the challenge from the community will continue to be very real and extremely conflicting at times. The more one can become educated for such a career, the better, although that alone will not resolve the dilemma created by a financially pinched community demanding better protection and greater crime prevention efforts from its police department.

Among the improvements that have been underway throughout the police service are better management techniques, wider use of computer assistance, more attention to performance evaluations, and considerable attention to training needs.

The 1980s witnessed improved professional status for the police officer in America. Educational requirements, communication skills, sophisticated training, and technological support enlarged the position and enhanced the image of the police officer considerably. It will always be recognized that the police force is on the cutting edge of violence and disorder and must possess the skills to confront these matters effectively. The physician does this in the emergency room of a hospital; so must the police officer make wise decisions quickly and under much pressure.

To summarize then, police protection in the United States was patterned after the English system and made little significant professional progress until the post–Civil War period. Gradually certain areas emerged as legal responsibilities of the states, and others became solely federal government functions. The student of police history will want to review the Pendleton Act to better understand police administration and how reform began to take effect in the form of civil service systems.

The student of issues relating to citizen control, community crime watch, and/or collective protection programs (even including the hiring of private forces) will surely want to review the writings on vigilante groups and "how the West was won" by such famed legends as Wild Bill Hickok, Wyatt Earp, and Bat Masterson.

Watchers of the presidential commissions should become familiar with the 1929 Wickersham Commission appointed by President Hoover, and the one appointed in 1967 by President Johnson. *The Challenge of Crime in a Free Society*, published along with a number of *Task Force Reports*, was the product of the President's Commission on Law Enforcement and Administration of Justice. Its many conclusions are very valuable contributions to the literature and led to the federal government's decision to distribute funds to assist in the control of crime. No one who really wants to understand the evolution of the police and the various situations that impact upon how the police operate can afford to ignore the writings that appear in these historic governmental documents.

It is interesting and quite revealing to note that professional literature, textbooks, and journals are largely products of the last fifty years. Thus, in little more than a generation, the profession of law enforcement has arisen, assembled its history, assessed its own status, enacted standards, adopted national recommendations, and clearly set its goals to be consistent with the same demands that are made of other long-established and recognized endeavors. There is now a truly recognized accreditation process.

The 1990s face many new challenges. By far, the involvement of communities, particularly their young people, with illegal drugs has created great pressures on police. The enforcement time allocated to dealing with the drug crisis overshadows much of the progress that has been made in modern policing. Drug sales, distribution, and usage virtually overwhelm some police jurisdictions and fill jails and prisons with those offenders. Street crimes and much family disintegration result from drug usage.

On the brighter side, police may expect considerable community support and involvement that ultimately should lead to certain crimes being reported and reduced. Which offenses these may be depends a great deal upon where the citizens put the pressure and whether new technology truly reduces incidents such as house burglaries and auto thefts. Of course, technology and the age of computers may also herald an entirely new array of criminal schemes and international terrorism that will affect American citizens.

PERSONNEL NEEDS

Few occupations in the public service field offer as challenging and varied a career as law enforcement. Whether at the federal, state, or local level, employment opportunities continue to grow because of population expansion and social complexities. Undoubtedly the police of the world have emerged from a history of uncertainty as to their proper functions, but in the United States, as representatives of all citizens, they are responsible for maintaining peace and order within the framework of the law. The police role is changing rapidly and is enjoying greater stature and prestige than ever before.

In years past, requirements for police officers, also called peace officers, were not as rigid. The service was not effectively competing for educated young people. More recently, partly because of community concern about crime and disorder, law enforcement finds itself on the threshold of professional status and its career appeal increasing. The urgency and importance of policing was described by the President's Commission on Law Enforcement and Administration of Justice in its special *Task Force Report* [on the] *Police*:

> The police . . . are the part of the criminal justice system that is in direct daily contact both with crime and with the public. The entire system—courts and corrections as well as the police—is charged with enforcing the law and maintaining order. What is distinctive about the responsibility of the police is that they are charged with performing these functions where all eyes are upon them and where the going is roughest, on the street.

According to the U.S. Bureau of Justice Statistics, there are more than 12,000 local police departments at the city, township, and municipal levels of government. Surprising to many Americans, and most certainly amazing to foreigners, is that three-fourths of those departments operate with fewer than twenty-five sworn officers. Looking at this same statistic from other viewpoints, about 8 percent of the sheriff's departments employ more than 100 sworn deputies. Of the nation's local police departments, some 15 percent have between 25 and 100 sworn officers, and actually less than 1 percent of either local police or sheriff's departments have 500 or more officers. In other words, policing in America is very much a function of local communities and modest-sized organizations.

In 1993 there were an estimated 766,126 employees, including 553,773 sworn officers, in local police and sheriff's departments. The overall law enforcement employment rate was 3.1 per 1,000 inhabitants; but only a 2.3 rate when considering full-time sworn officers.

There are recommendations to consolidate some of these smaller units, often through a contract with other larger communities or the sheriff's agency. In fact, in the past several years, the actual number of municipal police agencies has declined somewhat because of an increase in contractual arrangements, consolidation efforts, and other attempts to streamline and economize the numbers of different organizations. Some of the nonmunicipal departments would be the county police agencies found in some states, housing and port authorities, townships, special districts, and school districts. Even park police may be a separate and special unit. In addition to the county sheriffs, there are forty-nine independent cities that have a sheriff because of a consolidated city-county form of government. Colleges and universities may operate their own police.

It should be noted that some county police departments are among the largest police organizations. Some examples are the Los Angeles Sheriff's Office with 7,900 sworn; Nassau County, New York, with 3,000; Baltimore County, Maryland, with 1,500 sworn; and Dade County Police (Florida) with 2,600.

Further examples of the total sworn officer strengths in some major cities will help demonstrate how large local police departments can be. By far, the largest American police agency is in New York City, where the Housing Police Authority, the Transit Police, and the local department all combine to total some 38,000 officers. These personnel cover subways, housing developments, the boroughs, and the parks. Chicago has 12,600 sworn at this writing. Los Angeles City Police has more than 8,000 officers; Philadelphia has 7,000; Detroit almost 5,000; and Houston has 4,700 officers. Those city departments showing sworn staff over 2,000 include Washington, D.C., with 4,300; Baltimore with 3,000; Dallas with 2,800. Just under the 2,000 officer figure, one finds Boston with 1,900; Cleveland with 1,800; San Francisco with 1,900; St. Louis with 1,600; Kansas City with 1,200; and Phoenix with 1,900. Some large cities, like New York and Chicago, had larger organizations, but municipal budget reductions resulted in losses of personnel.

What figures such as these say to the young person seeking a career is that opportunities exist throughout the nation in police work, but greater numerical vacancies will be found in the larger cities and heavily populated suburban counties that often surround the large city. Thirty-four departments have more than a thousand officers.

Many people prefer working in the communities other than the very largest urban complexes. For them, the options are many. Middle range cities have police departments numbering 1,000 plus. For example,

Cincinnati has 971 officers as of our latest data. New Orleans reports 1,500 sworn officers during this time period and Jacksonville, Florida, has 1,200 sworn officers. Atlanta, Georgia, has 1,600 sworn, Honolulu has 2,000 officers, and Seattle has 1,250.

That law enforcement employment rate has increased to 3.6 in the populated cities with 250,000 or more inhabitants when we consider the total personnel data. Suburban county agencies averaged 3.6 employees per 1,000 inhabitants.

Furthermore it should also be understood that civilian employment within law enforcement has been increasing. In 1973 civilians made up 14.6 percent of all police personnel. By the 1987 data civilians made up 25 percent of the total law enforcement employee force. The 1993 data indicate that civilians comprise 28 percent of employees. That dramatic increase over the decade suggests some noticeable alterations of the police work setting. Many civilian personnel are assigned to records, to communication units, to labs, to computers, and to planning work. In general this suggests greater effort at productivity by moving nonenforcement duties away from sworn officers. The message seems clear that one might consider working for a police department, but in a civilian capacity. For the rural law enforcement agencies, the civilian figure is 34 percent, again demonstrating a strong commitment to civilianize much of the work of our suburban police.

Nationwide, the 1993 data indicated that female officers have remained steady at about the 10 percent level. In other words, male officers still dominate by 90 percent the sworn positions across the country. Women are slightly less likely to work in the rural areas—only 7 percent, but in the suburban (county) agencies they were at 12 percent.

In Los Angeles, a forerunner in the employment of women officers, the number has reached about 14 percent with many women now in supervisory ranks and some in command ranks. Much national media publicity has been given to several cities where women have reached the top executive level and served as chief of police.

There are cities where the figure is higher because they have sought to employ women over a period of time and have distributed assignments on an equitable basis. Some of the noteworthy cities in this regard are Washington, D.C.; Miami, Florida; New York City; Atlanta, Georgia; Indianapolis, Indiana; and Detroit, Michigan. Madison, Wisconsin may hold the record for gender equity, since 25 percent of that police department are women. And among the nation's largest cities, Detroit tops the list with 19 percent being female. In certain large cities, where the strong equal employment efforts have been concentrated, the hiring of female officers will be much greater. No longer do female officers work only in communications, dispatching, clerical, records, property rooms, or as jail matrons. They are found in patrol cars and on detective assignments and in supervisory and command ranks as well. The National Sheriff's Association reports that there are eleven female sheriffs in the country. A career female officer recently became chief of detectives in the Los Angeles County Sheriff's Department, one of the nation's largest police agencies.

Female officers are really not new; they were hired in Los Angeles in 1910 for patrol work involving women and children. Major changes began to occur during the late 1960s and early 1970s, when Washington, D.C., became one of the first to employ patrolwomen in large numbers and for similar duties as men. However, it is important to note that many communities did have female police officers during the 1930–1960 era. To be sure, many had specialized assignments dealing with crime prevention and delinquency matters, but it was not uncommon for women to be given duties involving the investigation of crimes affecting the community well being.

Again, as with employment generally, chances for women in police work are greatest in the largest cities. In 1983 the percentage of female officers in cities over one million in population was 6.1 percent; in cities of half million up to one million there were 7 percent female officers. More recent data show slight increases. As one looks to the smaller cities and small towns this figure decreases to around 4 percent, but interestingly, increases again to 12 percent for rural and suburban counties, reflecting opportunities in county police and sheriff's departments. It should be pointed out for those not interested in sworn positions that the female employment percentages in all agencies for civilian jobs are significantly higher, as much as 60 percent.

In addition to careers at the local level, data now indicate that 15 percent of military police officers are female. Likewise, agencies such as the FBI and the Secret Service have recruited women for more than a decade now. The earliest state police units to recruit women include Pennsylvania and Maryland. Young women interested in police careers should seek out and speak with those who have achieved this career goal. *Breaking & Entering; Policewomen on Patrol,* by Susan E. Martin (published by the University of California, Berkeley Press, paperback, 1982), is a book highly recommended for those who wish to locate a detailed study of this subject. Another recent resource is *The Status of Women in Policing,* also by Susan E. Martin (Police Foundation Report, Washington, DC, 1990).

FUTURE OUTLOOK

New appointments must continue as estimates consistently place the number of entry level positions available at thirty thousand. Some others view this as a conservative estimate based upon traditional population and economic growth projections. The rise in crime and the public and political concern for public safety as the population grows will always dictate a positive employment situation for jobs in police work. Retirements of those who entered in the post–World War II period are long over and likewise, those with Korean conflict duty have now served out their twenty-five- or thirty-year careers. Governmental budget tightening and reduced population expansion must be balanced against the turnover and the demands for new services.

The United States Department of Labor's *Occupational Outlook Handbook* states that the kinds of police jobs that arise in the future are likely to be affected to a considerable degree by the changes now taking place in enforcement methods and equipment. Specialists are becoming more and more essential, and there will be a greater need for officers with training ranging from engineering techniques applied to traffic control to social work techniques applied to crime prevention. Furthermore, as statistical analysis and data utilization increase, there are expanding needs for computer technicians, data analysts, and long-range planners. In addition, such new concepts as the *state specialist*, recommended by the National Advisory Commission on Criminal Justice Standards and Goals, will enhance career opportunities in this field. All states have developed state investigative specialty units to assist local law enforcement agencies with crimes that require special investigative knowledge. The majority of these programs have been implemented for such specific problems as organized crime, consumer protection violations, or violent hate crimes or serial murders.

In summary, law enforcement is one of the largest career groups dealing in public service. Because of our system of government, opportunities exist throughout all jurisdictions. At the federal level, our government employs many thousands of investigative agents and specialists in departments such as Justice, Treasury, and Defense. The fifty states employ both civilian and sworn personnel in agencies known as either state police or highway patrols. At the local level, where the vast number of career opportunities exist, there are sheriff's departments and municipal police agencies. Some areas of the country also have county police departments, and many communities employ village, township, and borough police. And they exist, literally, in the thousands! Every so often, one will learn of a newly established police agency when voters determine to annex their own municipality and undertake a more local form of public safety.

Federally funded initiatives assisted communities to obtain support for hiring additional police during the mid-1990s and the downsizing of military units has generated federally supported programs to place former servicemen and servicewomen into local police careers. In the first one and one-half years of the federal hiring support program, more than $1.5 billion dollars had been provided to employ more than 25,000 police officers and sheriff's deputies throughout the nation.

In the years ahead much greater public attention will be called to police tasks that require considerable professional skills. In the past, the many challenges facing law enforcement have not been apparent and have been little understood by the public. Police status and pay have increased significantly, and educational achievements have been remarkable. Probably no single career group in history has ever achieved so much higher education in so short a time as has the American law enforcement officer. Much of this is due to a federally funded program known as the Law Enforcement Education Program (LEEP), 1968–1980.

Most enforcement functions and duties cannot change overnight because the primary concern of the police is to protect the public. The police department is the twenty-four-hour agency best equipped to respond to requests for aid. Nonetheless, many dramatic changes in assignments and procedures have occurred in recent years, and authorities generally agree that the role of the police in American society is moving rapidly toward closer involvement in community-based programs, with greater emphasis on crime prevention. Recently, the police have become particularly active in efforts aimed at specific offense reduction through programs to harden frequent targets, encourage greater use of locks and alarms, and, in general, advise homeowners and the business community about crime risks. In the years ahead, the enforcement officer must display greater insight into community problems, social sciences, conflict resolutions, and the complex factors that contribute to unlawful activities.

No one can predict entirely to what extent policing will change as more data become computerized and the agencies become more involved with community planning and crime prevention. It is safe to assume, however, that competent personnel will be in demand and that training and education have become an integral part of the system. As in other professions, job descriptions will reflect a variety of tasks according to the level of career preparation. Future duties and salaries of police officers are beyond our estimates today, but policing is being acknowledged as deserving of full professional recognition, with rigid state licensing for those who practice its calling.

Much attention has been focused upon the police officer in America and the tremendous task of maintaining order. A great deal is being researched and written currently about the role of the police, but there is little doubt that the police provide one of the most essential, and often one of the least appreciated, services that exist anywhere. Few can dispute the importance of the men and women who must enforce our laws, prevent disorder, investigate offenses, and keep the peace. Without their efforts and constant vigilance, the daily routine of all of us would be in jeopardy, and through their continuous presence, most of us live the greater part of our lives free from attack or theft.

Despite frequent pressures and frustrations, the police service offers career opportunities unmatched in other vocations for those young people who prefer working with a variety of circumstances in an unpredictable environment. The demands of the job are great: there are stresses and temptations, long hours and interrupted plans, weekends are just more work days, and many shifts end with the officer feeling unable to maintain order for eight hours in even one patrol area. This knowledge could affect work efficiency, so it is important that the applicant for such a career accept the realities of dealing with human problems. He or she must be able to accomplish the duties with emotional resilience. Consider the comments of a prominent psychologist who has studied police officers and their behavior:

> Reviewing the tasks we expect of our law enforcement officers, it is my impression that their complexity is perhaps greater than that of any other profession. On the one hand, we expect our law enforcement officer to possess the nurturing, caretaking, sympathetic, empathic, gentle characteristics of physician, nurse, teacher, and social worker as he deals with school traffic, acute illness and injury, juvenile delinquency, suicidal threats, and missing persons. On the other hand, we expect him to command respect, demonstrate courage, control hostile impulses, and meet great physical hazard.... He is to control crowds, prevent riots, apprehend criminals, and chase after speeding vehicles. I can think of no other profession which constantly demands such seemingly opposite characteristics.*

Law enforcement is one of the largest of the semiprofessional occupational groups. It is striving for professional status, and as the more progressive agencies continue to contribute new achievements, the opportunities for greater service expand. Here is how another noted authority on criminal justice described events some twenty years ago.

> More police will be employed to keep pace with society. Professionalism will increase through greater stress on training. The trend toward more highly educated officers is inevitable. In order to accomplish this, higher pay scales will develop in a highly competitive job market. The criteria for selection will be modified to take advantage of evolving techniques that will measure more accurately the potential of candidates for law enforcement work....
> More electronic equipment will be utilized....New technology also will aid in solution of problems of police deployment.
> ...there will certainly be more sharing of such personnel as burglary, arson, and homicide specialists. Training, communications, records, criminal laboratories, and correctional institutions will be increasingly specialized and merged to create overall efficiency.**

The career aspirant must recognize that law enforcement is not a single job or one particular assignment. The field encompasses a broad

---

*Dr. Ruth Levy, Peace Officers Research Project, National Institute of Mental Health Grant, San Jose, California.

**Felkenes, George T. *The Criminal Justice System: Its Functions and Personnel.* Englewood Cliffs, NJ: Prentice-Hall, 1973, pp. 35–36.

spectrum of functions and cannot be described as one in which certain characteristics are essential and others unimportant. The need for police professionals is extremely great; the opportunities for capable young people are unlimited. Police now enjoy greater respect and status. Few careers can be more satisfying in terms of helping one's fellow human beings, and none offers a more exciting challenge.

In the most recent federal government survey, violent crime headed the list of workload problems that police chiefs and sheriffs said they faced. Most indicated their department's response took the form of community policing strategies. What is it that contributes to violent crimes? The response was domestic violence—assault, abuse, and the like. Furthermore 95 percent of all chiefs and sheriffs said that drug possession and sales were creating workload problems because of the increase in number of cases. Likewise 83 percent stated that crimes committed with firearms contributed to these workload problems—the availability of firearms to juveniles also was stressed.

By the 1990s new terms were being applied to some earlier concepts and team policing and community relations became known as problem-solving policing, community policing, and neighborhood focused policing. Many asked if the police were simply revisiting the "old-fashioned beat officer" of the past.

However the definitions may prevail, the job is truly a fascinating one, and priorities tend to be with crime prevention, conflict resolution, tension reduction, and a pro-active effort aimed toward maintaining peace and security for all.

CHAPTER 2

JOBS AT THE CITY
AND COUNTY LEVELS

Counseling for a career choice in law enforcement varies rather extensively, depending upon the jurisdictional level at which one is interested in joining. The federal agencies are easier to apply for, in the sense that a single office furnishes information and applications and affords the applicant centralized procedural steps. Likewise at the state level, whether it be a state police or a highway patrol, there would be a central headquarters responsible for all personnel matters. It is at the local level, where the greatest number of opportunities exist, that no one procedure or process is available. Once an individual has made the decision to seriously consider entering this exciting and challenging field, contact should be made with the department in which the applicant is interested in order to obtain its specific requirements. However, this book will attempt to describe the entrance process generally found throughout city and county police agencies.

PERSONAL REQUIREMENTS

Although it may seem a relatively simple matter, the serious applicant should not take the initial formal job application lightly. It is often designed to test one's ability to follow instructions, to provide details, and to be honest and thorough. The background investigation will prevail, so applicants should be complete in reporting their life's experiences. The best advice is to not try to hide a poor traffic record in another state, or a minor involvement with authorities while in one's teenage years. Above all, do not leave blanks on the application or fail to provide details when requested. Agencies' first impressions will be based largely upon that application form.

In addition to the questions about oneself, a written application will contain questions regarding relatives, personal and business references, military service, and formal schooling. Quite possibly the applicant will also be asked to state reasons for being interested in a law enforcement career with that particular organization. United States citizenship is required by all law enforcement agencies. A large number of departments have eliminated prior residency requirements of the police applicant, although by no means have they been totally removed. State residency may be required prior to employment, but the trend now is to invite applications from any area of the United States. Once hired, an employee may be required to reside within a given city or county.

In the United States, entrance age requirements now range from a minimum of 21 (in some jurisdictions, 19) to a maximum of 35 years, although some departments may hire applicants up until age 40. In certain circumstances, high school graduates may obtain employment through a cadet program. The cadet program allows individuals to be employed before their twenty-first birthday, and it also provides for consideration of employment as a police officer upon reaching the twenty-first birthday. Cadet programs have enabled young persons to become acquainted with the police field through various nonenforcement tasks. An applicant might consider making formal application prior to age 21, as the process itself takes some time, and there are departments that permit the submission of applications as much as one year in advance. Also, there are departments that allow entrance into the training program if the recruit will become 21 years old while training is in progress. Several major departments, notably Miami, Houston, Dallas, and Philadelphia, some years ago began to accept candidates under the age of 21, even authorizing them for street duty. This recruiting procedure may continue to expand. Also, as lateral transfers continue, there will be more opportunity to enter one department up to age 40 when the applicant has had prior police experience elsewhere.

All police departments require applicants to be of good moral character, emotionally stable, and mature. A serious criminal record, particularly conviction, will be the basis for rejection. Serious prior traffic violations, especially as an adult, could also result in disqualification, since possession of a valid driver's license is required. All applicants are given a thorough background investigation that will determine their integrity, reliability, and sobriety. The applicant's habits, conduct, and reputation in the community will be evaluated. Additional screening may also include one or a series of psychological tests, with or without accompanying interviews. Some police departments utilize psychiatrists to test and interview applicants, but this has proven costly and no more effective than psychological assessments. A polygraph examination may be required, and a personal interview is a certainty.

SELECTION REQUIREMENTS

Traditional selection criteria recently have been reexamined in light of concerns for equal opportunity. Much of the controversy developed after research indicated that minority group members had disadvantages in written test situations and in meeting what were arbitrary physical requirements. Police personnel procedures, especially selection practices, are based frequently on a civil service or merit system and standards set by the police department. A number of cooperative arrangements are under way to develop more universally effective procedures for selection.

In 1971 a national study conducted by the International Association of Chiefs of Police (IACP) reported great variations in requirements. These data indicated that differences in opinions exist, and little had been proven in the past regarding pre-employment standards and their relation to later career success. Although there are still jurisdictional variations, a standard system encompassing selection, recruit training, and probationary field performance has proved most acceptable. Although some standards still vary, they are all now far more likely to be job related.

A good source of information on police selection is *Police Personnel Practices in State and Local Governments* by the International Association of Chiefs of Police. This publication describes personnel management trends, as agencies respond to changing employment conditions and job requirements, and it includes specific discussions on employment of female and minority personnel, recruitment, performance appraisal, and lateral transfer. Communities and personnel departments now often contract with firms for written tests that are valid and nondiscriminatory.

Written Tests

Written tests are common and practical, since they can be easily administered and scored and are very economical. During the 1970s, written entrance exams were challenged legally as not being reflective of all cultures and genders, and much research has gone into making such tests job based, bias free and universally acceptable. Thorough job-task analysis has made entrance tests widely used and generally more reliable and valid. One can definitely expect a lengthy written examination when seeking public safety employment. In fact, far more applicants take such tests than ever obtain employment, and some agencies consider the stress and experience of undergoing the test and following instructions as the first of many application hurdles to becoming an officer. Regardless of the type of written test the applicant may encounter, the following skills will always improve applicants' abilities to express themselves in writing: reading comprehension, analytical ability, self-expression, and capacity to retain details, recall events, and make decisions based upon facts.

All departments now require successful completion of high school, although various alternatives do exist, such as certification through the Armed Services Institute or equivalency examinations (GED) by a state department of education. Applicants are not generally required to be knowledgeable about law enforcement prior to their employment, but an applicant with advanced academic knowledge in the field may reasonably be expected to be better qualified for such employment.

Physical Examinations

Police service at any level of government requires physically sound personnel. Severe physical exertion is called for occasionally, and the applicant, male or female, must possess the stamina to work for long periods of time without rest.

Minimum medical standards have been established and observed by most departments. Generally, any marked deformity, overweight condition, or weak muscular development may result in disqualification. Hearing and visual acuity must be within acceptable limits, although most departments permit corrective lenses to be worn. Thus far, the courts have paid little attention to standards related to vision and general physical health, since these are reasonably job related. Generally speaking, eyesight must be correctable to 20/20 and no color blindness is permitted.

Minimum height and weight requirements had become the subject of controversy, and height and weight standards are being made more flexible in order to include a more representative group of applicants. However, the medical examination still prevails and weight must be in proportion to height, although the minimum height standard clearly has been lowered.

Of course anyone seeking a police appointment must undergo a complete medical examination. This often is requested early in the process, since certain physical conditions do account for a significant number of rejections. Blood pressure, heart conditions, lack of required strength and agility, and inadequate coordination skills can all result in medical rejection. Furthermore recent evidence of drug usage will disqualify the applicant. Urinalysis will be required by most agencies to determine current status of alcohol and drugs in the body. The more stringent agencies will require urinalysis during the medical screening, during the academy training, and perhaps following the training, prior to assignments.

Certain physical agility requirements do relate to the enforcement occupation, but rather than the more traditional skills appraised through exercise-type tests, research has now determined what kinds of physical skills are essential to the job. Some most likely to be retained have to do with lifting and arm strength, the ability to drive a car, fire a weapon, disarm an assailant, and swim. Although physical agility tests may continue to vary throughout the country, their presence indicates that many physicians and civil service boards believe that a police applicant should be able to perform rigorous physical activities at an average or above average level, and mere evidence of good health will not be sufficient for employment. A job analysis conducted in the Miami, Florida, region has resulted in the following recommended procedures regarding the administering of physical agility exams. The exam for police applicants is to measure accomplishment of the following: run short distance, run assist officer, run subdue suspect, climb stairs, grip strength (weapon related), push disabled vehicle, climb six-foot chain link fence, carry fifty pounds, climb through window, climb onto roof using ladder, demonstrate modest swimming abilities. A 1993 research study from IACP expanded this list to include bending and reaching, using force, using devices for restraints, and possessing body flexibility.

Personal Interview

One almost unanimous requirement among enforcement agencies is some form of personal interview, and this can be of great importance. The interview board generally consists of several representatives from the police department, as well as someone from the personnel department of the employing jurisdiction. Interview lengths vary considerably, but the questions tend to revolve around the applicant's past work experience, education, personal history and characteristics, and reasons for choosing police work as a career. An applicant should bear in mind that the board will not only be judging responses to questions, but also personal appearance and manner. Of particular importance will be the applicant's expression of interest in a police career and intention to pursue it in a dedicated way.

Quite understandably, all police agencies require that a character or background investigation be conducted on each applicant. This is a time-consuming and costly procedure and almost always occurs toward the end of the selection process. Thus, this effort would not be expended on applicants who had failed to qualify on previous criteria. It is important that the candidate furnish as much detail as possible so this investigation can be performed without unnecessary delays. As an example, complete names, titles, addresses, and phone numbers of references should be furnished. All previous employment and residence locations must be accurate, and an applicant should remember that he or she is being evaluated by the information furnished. Failure to include all pertinent data or to account for time periods may cause serious delay and even rejection. If an applicant spent time in the military or in college, and there are brief time intervals when neither was the primary activity, the time gap should be explained. If you believe the application process is appealing, and that you can successfully meet the rather stringent requirements, then a law enforcement career may be for you. But before you decide, consider those abilities that research has established as critical to the tasks performed by police officers. Whether they are analyzed through written exams, personal and group interviews, medical analyses, psychological screening, polygraph tests, assessment center exercises, psychiatric interviews, and/or agility and motor ability demonstrations, these traits have survived the research and must be possessed by the applicant:

Leadership. Initiate action, independently assume control of a situation; obtain information from others; direct, assist, and provide guidance to others.

Maturity. Display courtesy and consideration for the problems, needs, and feelings of others in a fair manner; use discretion in exercising police authority.

Perception. Identify and understand the critical elements of a situation; observe situational details and conditions; recognize discrepancies or circumstances that require action; interpret the implications of such actions.

Good Judgment. Use logical and sound judgment when responding to a situation based upon a recognition and understanding of the facts available; define problem situations and initiate actions based upon established guidelines and procedures.

Decisiveness. Willingly take action and make decisions based upon situational need; render judgments; willingly defend actions or decisions when confronted by others.

Adaptability. Be flexible when dealing with situations involving change; appropriately modify a course of action as the situation changes; maintain constructive behavior despite time pressures, or pressures exerted by others.

Oral Communication. Clearly express oneself through oral means: properly used grammar, vocabulary, eye contact, and voice inflection.

Written Communication. Clearly and effectively communicate relevant information in writing, use accurate vocabulary and proper grammar and spelling.

The above described characteristics are the result of research conducted at the Dade-Miami (Florida) Assessment Center for entry-level police officers, which identified and grouped 102 specific skills and abilities required of the entry-level police officer. Similar research has been conducted under Project Star (System Training & Analysis of Requirements for Criminal Justice Participants) over a period of three years in four states (California, Texas, Michigan, and New Jersey). Further findings regarding job task analysis were reported by the National

Planning Association (Washington, D.C.) during its National Manpower Survey. These two major federally funded studies were produced during the period 1971–1976 and represented the most extensive review of personnel selection and training ever presented to this field. Students of criminal justice interested in matters relating to manpower development would be well advised to obtain these reports from college or agency libraries. Based on such prior research, some states utilize a commercial vendor to administer a standard entry exam.

Polygraph-Lie Detector Examinations

Over the years this particular selection technique has varied in emphasis. Presently it is in wide usage among agencies because of the increased illegal drug problem in the country. Typical previous usage of the polygraph was limited to exploring thefts from employers, being removed from prior employment, and situations dealing with use of other's property. Currently the emphasis in polygraph examinations is on prior and continuing use of illegal drugs. The type of drug, extent of the usage, and the time interval since that usage are all factors that will be considered.

PROBATION, TENURE, AND PROMOTION

The length of the probation period after employment is usually one year, and two years at the most. After serving the probationary period successfully, the majority of departments ensure job security, except for cases in which formal charges are brought against the employee.

Very few differences exist among most law enforcement agencies with regard to promotion. Likewise, most agencies have a stated, formalized promotion program. Generally seniority in a particular rank is among those items considered in promoting an employee. An oral interview also is conducted, along with an evaluation of general service experience in the department. In addition, to attain most ranks, there may well be a written examination and some type of job performance assessment. Formal performance appraisals will be conducted as often as every month, or at least quarterly. Even if such personnel activity evaluations are only semi-annual, they provide valuable insights about an individual's ability to do the job.

Performance evaluations typically review the officer's skill as measured by a number of events. These might include arrests, court convictions, persons interviewed in the course of patrol duties, cases investigated, reports filed, and numerous other categories. Any citizen complaints formally charged against the officer, and likewise any commendations, would also be considered; so might attitude, appearance, and professional demeanor.

In recent years, articulate, better-educated officers have done exceptionally well in front of the oral interview board, and promotions may well continue to occur in this manner until higher education becomes an integral part of the requirements for promotion. In some of the more progressive agencies, there are now assessment centers where simulated exercises, role playing, and objective reviews that assist in the promotional process are conducted. They do not necessarily replace written examinations or oral interviews, but they are a very useful method for making impartial comparisons among candidates for a position, and they are based upon actual behavioral events, and not just test scores. To the extent that the simulations are designed to resemble actual job demands and expectations, the assessment center may become the process for the future in selecting finalists for promotions in rank.

THE PATROL OFFICER

Who is the police patrol officer? What tasks are performed and what skills must one have? Again, to quote from the President's Commission on Law Enforcement and Administration of Justice in the special *Task Force Report* [on the] *Police*:

> The heart of the police effort against crime is patrol—moving on foot or by vehicle around an assigned area, stopping to check buildings, to survey possible incidents, to question suspicious persons, or simply to converse with residents who may provide intelligence as to occurrences in the neighborhood.
>
> The object of patrol is to disperse police in a way that will eliminate or reduce the opportunity for misconduct and to increase the likelihood that a criminal will be apprehended while he is committing a crime or immediately thereafter. The strong likelihood of apprehension will presumably have a strong deterrent effect on potential criminals. The fact of

apprehension can lead to the rehabilitation of a criminal, or at least to his removal for a time from the opportunity to break the law.

When patrol fails to prevent a crime or apprehend a criminal, the police must resort to investigation. Some investigation is carried out by patrol officers, but the principal responsibility rests with detectives. Investigation aims at identifying offenders through questioning victims, suspects, witnesses and others, through confronting arrest suspects with victims or witnesses, through photographs, or less frequently, through fingerprints or other laboratory analysis of evidence found at crime scenes.

Patrol is high on police management's list of priorities because most departments spend ninety percent of their budget for personnel and as much as sixty percent of their budget on patrol personnel specifically. Further strengthening the significance of patrol, the National Advisory Commission on Standards and Goals has recommended that every police administrator ensure maximum efficiency in the delivery of patrol services, including immediate response to incidents, an emphasis on the need for preventive patrol to reduce the opportunity for criminal activity, and the placement of a priority upon each request for police service.

Not only is patrol the backbone of the crime prevention effort, it is also the foundation of the greatest part of all community contact and communication. The patrol officer is the everyday representative of the law enforcement agencies to the community at large and has the greatest impact upon community life.

The International Association of Chiefs of Police developed the following job description for the police patrol officer:

General Duties

Is responsible through the enforcement of laws and ordinances for the protection of life and property in an assigned area during a specific period. Performs routine police assignments received from officers of superior ranks; conducts preliminary investigations; assists in the apprehension of criminals. Also performs special assignments requiring specialized skills or abilities.

Distinguishing Features of the Class

This work consists primarily of routine patrol tasks. Work may involve elements of danger and does involve many emergencies which demand that the employee must be able to exercise sound judgment and act without direct supervision. However, procedures and special assignments are usually carried out under immediate supervision.

Illustrative Examples of Work

Patrols a specific area in a patrol car, to preserve law and order, to prevent and discover the commission of crime, and to enforce parking and traffic regulations. Required to make close inspection of actual or potential hazards to the public safety.

Responds to complaints concerning automobile crashes, robberies, and other minor and major violations of law.

Interviews persons making complaints and inquiries and attempts to make proper disposition or direct them to proper authorities.

Investigates suspicious activities and makes arrests for violations of federal and state laws and local ordinances.

Watches for and makes investigations of wanted and missing persons and stolen cars and property.

Conducts preliminary investigations.

Administers first aid at the scenes of accidents and crimes.

Maintains order in crowds.

Answers questions and directs the public.

Performs periodic safety and crime prevention tasks as community requirements dictate.

Ensures the rights of all citizens are protected and intervenes in disputes and disturbances to reduce their risk of becoming a crisis.

Required Knowledges, Skills, and Abilities

Good general intelligence and emotional stability.

Good judgment.

Ability to analyze situations quickly and objectively and to determine the necessary and proper action.

Ability to understand and carry out complex oral and written directions.

Good powers of observation and memory.

Ability to compose and legibly write or print complete factual reports.

A good knowledge of first aid methods, after training.

Ability to speak effectively.

Ability to drive a car.

Excellent moral character.

Excellent physical condition.
Physical strength and agility.
Skill in the use and handling of firearms, after training.

More recent texts list such duties as the following as primary responsibilities of a police officer:

1. Protect life and property.
2. Resolve interpersonal conflict and preserve the peace.
3. Maintain social order.
4. Prevent crime by proactive patrol and other measures.
5. Repress crime through effective law enforcement.
6. Create and perpetuate a sense of security.
7. Identify and apprehend those who have broken the law.
8. Regulate various types of noncriminal behavior.
9. Recognize and deal with police/public safety hazards.
10. Facilitate the movement of people and motor vehicles.
11. Provide essential emergency services.
12. Help those individuals who cannot care for themselves.
13. Safeguard legal and constitutional rights of citizens.

Let us look into this job description in detail and discuss just what the police officer does. We cannot describe all the assignments, but some common experiences are presented. It should also be noted that although the job information was written previously, it remains accurate today and provides some assurance that the police service does not change the basic duties to be performed. In fact, the core mission seems permanent.

As indicated in the President's Commission on Law Enforcement and Administration of Justice in the special *Task Force Report* (on the) *Police*, an officer patrols a particular area or neighborhood on foot or by vehicle. While on patrol, safe response to calls for assistance from the general public is a primary responsibility. These calls may be initiated from police headquarters or directly by a citizen. In either case, what the police officer does after arriving at the scene largely depends upon what has happened and how much information is available at that moment.

First the officer may find it necessary to hear a report from the victim of a crime or accident or from witnesses who observed the incident. The next course of action may be placing someone under arrest or entering the information obtained into a report for later investigation. Depending on the situation, the patrol officer may be called upon to preserve the peace through some immediate action or observe some piece of evidence that must be preserved and recorded. If an arrest is made, the suspect must be transported to the police station for the booking process. Enforcement personnel also assist the injured citizen in making a formal complaint. In the more serious cases, duties will include not only protecting the scene of the crime and obtaining information from witnesses, but also telling the detectives how the crime occurred and giving them any available clues.

In the case of an accident, the police officer's duties involve rendering first aid, calling for an ambulance, preventing further damage, noting all pertinent facts, and obtaining statements from those involved as well as any witnesses. Of course all of these matters necessitate a detailed recording and reporting of events.

The officer must also provide assistance in times of emergency such as fires or other catastrophes. Police assistance is not only sought during major calamities; it may consist of hundreds of requests for miscellaneous services: a domestic animal in trouble, a citizen in some distress, a lost child or elderly person, or such lost property as a bicycle, purse, or pet.

Often the police officer finds it necessary to issue traffic citations according to the motor vehicle code in the locale. Some violations may demand physical arrests, and, again, all will require full reporting of the action taken.

A great deal of time is devoted to observing and noting circumstances that could lead to more serious situations. Here the officer must identify *potential* hazards, whether they be neglect of children, the breeding of locations of vice, dangers to the personal safety of citizens, or any other conditions that might erupt into disorder or violence. Business locations also are inspected to reduce the likelihood of burglaries.

As one can readily see, little time is spent by police in making arrests, but once an arrest is made, it is necessary for the officer to appear in court. This calls for preparing notes and testimony that are accurate and relevant to the case. The officer must repeat conversations accurately and introduce exhibits and evidence in a professional, competent manner.

One of the most sensitive of the tasks that must be performed is the use of physical force to restrain someone who may assault an officer or another citizen. The patrol officer must always be prepared to repel violent assaults with proficient defensive tactics or the use of weapons and must also stay alert to prevent the escape of persons in custody.

In summary, when patrol officers are not engaged in riding patrol, answering emergency calls, handling citizen complaints, obtaining preliminary investigation information, making arrests, writing traffic citations and reports, or giving testimony in court, they are called upon by direct citizen contact on the street to deliver a variety of other services. Even beyond these duties, the officer will initiate action, upon individual judgment, without any direction from headquarters or other outside sources.

Automobiles are standard equipment for most police patrols in our country. A single uniformed officer in a marked patrol car is a familiar sight to everyone. Some circumstances demand that two officers ride patrol together, and communities generally find a combination of one- and two-officer vehicles to be the most appropriate policy. Few state police or deputy sheriffs patrol in pairs, but municipal officers handling numerous drunk or fight calls find it advantageous.

In recent years the motorized scooter has become useful in traffic work because it gets the police officer to the scene rapidly, unhampered by street congestion. Equipped with a walkie-talkie radio, the officer on a scooter is frequently in a position to confront a holdup or assault in progress.

Naturally, all of these methods may be used in varying degrees, depending upon the size of the community and demands made upon the department. A person choosing a police career can expect to spend much time in automobile patrol, but alternatives do exist. Flexibility is essential in delivering services to the public, and this variation has great appeal to most young people. In helicopters, in patrol boats, sometimes working with canine units, and occasionally still on horseback, patrol officers pursue their missions of enforcing laws, protecting citizens and their property, preventing crime and disorder, and ensuring the peace.

A police career aspirant should bear in mind that the daily work schedule will differ somewhat from that of neighbors and friends. It must be recognized that patrol is a twenty-four-hour-a-day activity and that it cannot be reduced on holidays or weekends, and, further, that many serious occurrences arise in the late evening and early morning hours. Beyond this, it must also be remembered that, because an officer is always a sworn protector of law and order, on-duty status is never really abandoned. One is subject to call to duty at any time, to overtime and extended shifts, and most enforcement personnel must devote a large amount of their time to completing the necessary reports and appearing in court.

Thus a tour of duty on patrol may close without headlines and may be relatively routine, but to the officer it may include hidden dangers, suspense, monotony, and a few moments of tension and excitement. An unpredictable time, such as a quiet Sunday morning, can bring holdup and homicide.

As we observed earlier, few major changes have really occurred in the basic patrol functions in modern times; technology has improved, record systems are rapid, and the training available to officers has increased immensely. But patrol still entails covering one's assigned area, preventing crime, and providing service. Officers today are more aware of constitutional rights, legitimate dissent, and the implications of taking official action, but fundamental responsibilities have not changed.

Everyone agrees that the core mission of the police is to control crime. In recent years, however, police response has been focused more exactly by screening the calls for service, targeting sections for patrol emphasis, and enhancing strategies for crime control that embrace some of the new technologies.

Community problem solving has become a more frequent police response than in the past. Organizing citizen groups and targeting the fear of crime has been given attention as an alternative to trying to respond to every call. Terms such as community policing, partnership with citizens, public accountability, and similar themes have been adopted rapidly by American police leaders, and the police are again being looked upon to deal with disorder and reduce fear about crime. Recent research shows that citizen fear of crime can be markedly reduced if police tactics increase the quality of police-citizen interaction. Police officers can also benefit from this interaction, as research shows that detective productivity can be enhanced if patrol officers obtain better information from neighborhood residents, and it is used efficiently.

Foot patrol has also been shown to reduce citizen fear and improve relationships between police and communities. In many communities, after decades of automobile patrol coverage, the police are returning to foot patrol. Foot patrol also shows evidence of increasing officers' satisfaction with their work because they are able to show reduction in certain crimes.

The 1990s will decide if community policing will survive. It is quite a different approach from the traditional one of efficient response to all needs. It is not incident or technology driven; officers are decentralized and must be in contact with citizens. It allocates police on the basis of neighborhoods, rather than being on-call and in-service to respond to anything.

Body armor has been introduced, vehicles are safer and more efficient, minicomputers can now report back answers to field officers, and today's average police officer enjoys some distinct personal advantages in salary progression, benefits and support. Nonetheless the job still demands intensity and alertness, and officers continue to find that crime-fighting duties consume far less time than do the service and protection functions that occupy their normal working hours.

However, one significant change is the steadily increasing numbers of women on patrol. The number of female officers has grown from 2–3 percent of sworn officers during the 1960–77 time period, to about 10–12 percent currently. More importantly, their duties have expanded from the original ones of dealing with delinquents, youth, female offenders, and staff support assignments, to the full array of patrol and investigative functions. The President's Commission on Law Enforcement and Administration of Justice, and more recently the National Advisory Commission on Criminal Justice Standards, recommended that police agencies ensure that policies permit qualified women to seek employment, and their usage not be limited to work with juveniles and youths. The commissions stated clearly that women should serve in patrol and investigative divisions, and that they should assume supervisory and administrative positions as they became qualified.

All of these recommendations were consistent with federal legislation under Title VII of the Civil Rights Act (1972), which prohibits discrimination by employers on the basis of race, creed, color, sex, or national origin. Hence, government agencies, including police departments, are required to prove that unless gender is a "bona fide occupational qualification," they must employ, assign, and advance women on the same basis as men. It is true today that many small departments may employ women in limited numbers, and many that initially employed them in support service roles have now advanced those women to sworn positions. And though it may still hold true that female officers are working in youth bureaus, community relations, vice, and family abuse cases, it is also equally true that there are many hundreds on patrol, many on duty as investigators, and some in supervisory and command ranks.

As more women are assimilated into the patrol units and gain experience as investigators and supervisors, they will possess the requirements for advancement and gain promotions. Within the past several years, major cities have promoted and assigned female police commanders to be in charge of a district or precinct. Often such a command has several hundred officers working within it.

One distinct advantage to females aspiring to police careers, which has held true throughout the entire history of their employment, has been equality in pay. Unlike many other occupations, a woman who completed the academy and was sworn in and assigned to duty, did receive the same pay and benefits as any other entry level police officer. In conjunction with legislative actions, a much greater awareness of career opportunities for women in criminal justice exists now. The implementation of more flexible entrance standards regarding height, weight, and strength has resulted in increased employment of women, and this will continue to occur. The expansion of duties, assignments, prestige, and authority will also continue.

Now that we have discussed in some detail the duties of the patrol officer, let us turn our attention to certain other categories of departmental assignments. Although one may seek or request certain types of assignments, it must always be remembered that the needs of the community, and the priorities of the agency, must come first. There is no real rule of thumb when it comes to specialized duty assignments: some are long-term by mutual agreement, some are short-term for a variety of reasons; but in nearly all instances, experience is a factor that remains important. Performance, of course, is another.

THE TRAFFIC OFFICER

The officer assigned to the traffic division or traffic bureau spends considerable time directing and controlling the flow of traffic. This function includes, of course, both motor vehicles and pedestrians. In addition to the traffic flow, the officer must be concerned with enforcing parking regulations, although sometimes this is handled by parking enforcement specialists, police cadets, or a specialized unit within the traffic division. Stolen or wanted automobiles are an important part of this unit's total responsibilities, and many such cars are located as a result of relatively minor traffic violations.

The traffic officer frequently is responsible for investigation of abandoned automobiles, as well as their removal. As in the traffic engineering division, reports must be made on the breakdown or inefficiency of traffic control devices.

A very important function of the police traffic specialist relates to the investigation of accidents. Not only must first aid be administered at the scene, but the traffic officer's reports are critical to explaining the causes of accidents and recommending any corrections that might be necessary to prevent future crashes. This may include such things as sign dimensions, obstructions to vision, engineering hazards, or driver inattention and bad habits.

The task of issuing traffic citations and making arrests of serious violators belongs to the entire police department, but traffic officers, particularly those on motorcycles, tend to give this greater priority. As in all other police assignments, the traffic enforcement officer spends time testifying in court and frequently becomes involved in civil cases arising out of traffic accidents. Motorist assistance, escort duty, crowd handling, and rerouting traffic all place great time demands on those officers concerned with traffic and highway safety. Traffic enforcement that is fair and efficient is very important in permitting all citizens to go about their daily routines.

THE DETECTIVE OR CRIMINAL INVESTIGATOR

Detective work in municipal departments typically begins where the activities of the patrol personnel end. It involves the continuation of investigations, apprehension of any offenders who have been identified, recovery of stolen properties, and again, the all-important tasks of completing official reports and preparing testimony and evidence for court presentation. Detectives do all follow-up interviewing, since the preliminary information-gathering process may have unconnected points in it and may require analysis that cannot be done easily at the initial scene by the patrol officer. Another critical task confronting the detective is the identification of the offender. This demands that one spend considerable time reviewing physical evidence, clues, interviews, files, background details of the event, and the offender's method of operation, with the ultimate goal of obtaining an identification.

In many ways the detective is a coordinator of investigations, utilizing the efforts of the patrol officers, laboratory personnel, computerized data and records, and affected citizens in the quest for accurate information.

Insofar as property is concerned, the detective must obtain a detailed inventory of all stolen items, including serial numbers, labels, markings, and any other distinctive data. The job of recovery requires contact with pawnshops and junkyards, as well as a few persons in the community who make their living through selling stolen articles. These people are popularly referred to as *fences*, and they often operate behind legitimate businesses.

Most detectives are assigned to that position, and departmental policy determines whether it is temporary or permanent. In some departments the detective status is acquired through examination, in addition to an impressive performance as a patrol officer. Sometimes detectives are rotated back to the patrol unit, and in some departments detective status is regarded as a promotion, thus becoming a permanent assignment, at least until the officer is promoted to a higher rank.

Any successful detective must possess these traits: energy, persistence, courage, initiative, resourcefulness, imagination, accurate memory, good judgment, and powers of observation. Some of these qualities may be gained through training and experience; others are an integral part of one's personality.

As a general rule, detectives specialize in certain kinds of offenses: crimes against *persons*—such as assault, homicide, rape, and robbery, and those against *property*—notably burglary, theft, and larceny. Detectives may likewise be assigned to juvenile delinquency and youth crimes, or to handling gangs and school-related offenses. There are also criminal investigative specialists in such technical areas as arson, auto theft, forgery, fraud, narcotics, and the more frequent illegal activities associated with vices (for example, gambling, prostitution, illegal beverages).

Such assignments involve long hours and demand patient and tireless effort, but also carry with them a somewhat higher pay scale, a clothing allowance, more flexible working hours, and greater freedom of activity. Also, the detective usually acquires a prestige that is especially attractive to young, ambitious patrol officers.

Team policing, the use of targeted patrol, and other modern approaches to better manpower utilization have attempted to combine the patrol function with that of the detective. Police departments are performing combined functions within a specific geographic area in this way by increasing employee responsibility and demanding accountability. Small groups of personnel enhance the opportunity for individual officer decision making enabling many departments to obtain better citizen cooperation and minimize the complexities of large organizations and mobile societies. For the educated officer the challenge is greater, since more personal autonomy can be exerted.

In the recent past much study and analysis has been conducted regarding how criminal investigations are prioritized and managed. Some agencies now use the patrol officer to a greater extent in the preliminary investigation, and even during follow-up work when it involves witnesses, records and files originating with the patrol officer, and informants. Future strategies will likely call for more targeted investigations in which cases are carefully screened, some are given priority, resources are more carefully managed, and emphasis is placed upon known, serious, and repeat offenders. A recent federal study provides insight for future policymaking by indicating that most robbery and burglary investigations are solved equally by criminal investigators and patrol officers, that such cases are conducted in a relatively short time span, that leads tend to dissolve after several days, and that the best sources of information are witnesses, informants, police records, and other police officers.

In addition to the specializations mentioned already, the size and demands of the agency will dictate the need for any others.

The following are some of the specialized assignments required in modern police service.

- Bomb and arson officers use specialized equipment and training to detect and disarm explosives or suspicious devices. They also investigate fires when the origin is in question.

- Canine officers are teamed with specially trained dogs to provide special skills in searches, tracking, and crowd control. Canine patrol units are in common usage everywhere.
- Community relations officers maintain contact and relationships between the police department and the community it serves. They are instrumental in crime prevention efforts and may provide linkage to schools, civic groups, and businesses as a part of their crime reduction and personal safety programs. School resource officers may be in this type of unit.
- Emergency services or tactical units are specially trained to perform rescues of various kinds. They are called to the scene of life-threatening events and have special equipment to facilitate their work. Special weapons and tactics teams support patrol units.
- Harbor patrol, helicopter, and short takeoff and landing aircraft are all a part of modern patrol work. Duties of those on such assignments will range from distress and rescue calls, to pursuit of smugglers and observation of ground activities for both safety and surveillance missions.
- Anticrime or street crime units work in high-crime areas and specialize in overt efforts to fight aggressive street crime. They may employ decoy tactics, stakeouts, or high visibility. Some may be assigned to gang control.
- Specialty units may exist for such purposes as dealing with juveniles and youths, sex crimes, vice and narcotics offenses, or any other criminal activities that require special attention. In recent years drug usage has compounded workloads.
- Additionally there are assignments to hostage negotiation teams, organized crime sections, intelligence-gathering, as well as internal affairs. And for those with the proper educational credentials, the training center or the academy may be a viable assignment.

When one considers further the potential for duty assignments to the training academy, property control, records and identification, laboratory with mobile units, and numerous other less-recognized but highly demanding areas of responsibility, it is easier to understand why law enforcement is regarded as a diverse and challenging occupation. Police agencies have legal advisors, researchers, data analysts, forensic scientists, computer programmers, and personnel specialists, all of whom could be police officers with long-term career assignments. Some of these could be civilians, too. A profile of the police would show a typical distribution similar to the following:

- 75 percent of all sworn personnel are line/patrol officers;
- 13 percent are management and command-level officers;
- 12 percent are first line supervisors, typically sergeants.

COUNTY UNITS AND SHERIFF'S DEPARTMENTS

Law enforcement career seekers may want to consider service at the county level of government. Some states have developed countywide police units that are organized and administered similarly to city departments. In such places patrol duties are the same as in the city department, except that the county employee may be responsible for a more extensive geographic area. Depending upon the population density, the county officer may find the duties similar to those of the state police officer. That is, a great variety of services will be performed while covering a broad geographic area, with many demands from the smaller communities and unincorporated sections. In several states, notably New York, Kentucky, Texas, Florida, Maryland, and Virginia, certain county police departments are regarded by authorities as some of the nation's finest examples of progress in maintaining law and order.

Often regarded as models of organization and performance, these same county departments have enjoyed very progressive leadership, with chiefs being appointed by the county executive or by a county board of commissioners. County police departments are not to be confused with sheriff's departments, although actual assignments and duties may not be very different. The sheriff is a constitutional officer and is historically and typically an elected official. The sheriff's office is found in most states where county police are not. The sheriff will possess some constitutional powers not generally assigned to the appointed police chief. Depending upon size of the population to be served, the sheriff will employ a force of uniformed deputies and, in many cases, plainclothes investigators. Since sheriffs are responsible for the administration of the county jail, they must also maintain a twenty-four-hour staff in that facility. As a general rule the sheriff's deputies perform patrol services, investigate offenses, and provide protection in the same manner as municipal law enforcement officers. The most significant difference, other than maintaining the county jail, is the sheriff's responsibility for serving civil papers and orders of the county courts and for transporting prisoners. In recent years sheriffs' departments have been able to move away from their historical fee system and adopt salary scales that are usually competitive with those of colleagues in the major cities. More recently the sheriffs have been able to secure civil service coverage for many of their employees, and while the sheriffs themselves must run for office in a popular election, many have succeeded in securing job protection for their deputies. Like the state police officer, the deputy sheriff can expect to be confronted by a variety of demands. Because such officers usually patrol alone, they must demonstrate resourcefulness and leadership. Deputy sheriffs are very much like their municipal counterparts; the significant difference is in the organization and jurisdiction of the agency itself.

With regard to the differences, deputy sheriffs often serve in the courtroom as bailiffs. They also may act as extradition officers for prisoner escorts, and serve orders or civil papers of the county court, including subpoenas, show-cause orders, property seizures, and garnishments. Some deputies are responsible for collecting legal fees assigned by the courts, some have jurisdiction in county parks and game areas, and currently, many have duty protecting court facilities and court officials. Some of the sheriff's departments that employ patrol services have contracted with smaller units of government, perhaps a township, and provide the police services for that community on the basis of the contract. In a circumstance such as this, often considered to be a progressive and productive arrangement, opportunities for employment may increase, although there may be fewer police agencies in the area.

One seeking a law enforcement career should certainly not overlook the many townships, boroughs, villages, and modest-sized cities that dominate this nation. Although this book tends to cite illustrations and activities most often identified with the more dense populations, the role of the police does not differ that much from a large urban center to a small village. The events to be responded to and the problems to be solved are often the same; what differs is the frequency with which they occur and the intensity with which the various demands arise. There are anticipated growths in personnel in many of the suburban and mid-sized towns as populations move out from the urban centers. This redistribution of police personnel is underway and promises to continue with annexations, contracting, consolidations, and rural America's insistence upon equal services.

Entrance qualifications and procedures, the desirability of higher education, the importance of training, the benefits and advantages of the job, and the potential for advancement and other careers, all will apply as much at the county level as in other areas of law enforcement. In fact recent and rapid population movements to the suburbs, the unincorporated areas, and the smaller communities on the periphery of large cities may increase potential for employment and expanded career choices at county agencies.

Law enforcement is making good strides toward greater officer discretion and a sense of personal accomplishment in police work. Whatever managerial techniques are employed, many progressive departments are encouraging and rewarding greater patrol officer responsibility and initiative. The labels will differ; team policing, community policing, master patrol officer, police agent, and various styles of beat coverage will apply; but the ultimate aim is to enhance a patrol officer's job and make it more desirable. Perhaps a combination of problem-solving patrol plus a four-day week!

Before concluding the discussion of local level police service, it might be timely to outline an ambitious and futuristic plan undertaken by the District of Columbia Metropolitan Police Department. For years the department has been doing some very proactive planning in order to improve its services. This planning reflects the thinking of the modern police agency and could well serve as a philosophical goal for those considering their own future in any police agency. Upon employment, all officers will receive orientation in the implementation of the concepts and exactly how operational improvements are to be brought about. In the meantime departmental task forces have established the plan, which consists of value and belief statements considered essential; these, in turn, provide all personnel with priorities, goals, and directions for the future:

- An improved capability to respond to citizen calls for service, particularly emergency calls requiring the immediate response of an officer.
- An improvement in the delivery of police services through more efficient and productive use of police officers' time while on duty.
- An increased ability to investigate crimes, particularly those crimes that have the greatest potential for being solved.
- An improved ability to identify and apprehend offenders.
- An increased understanding between the police and community regarding each other's problems and priorities through improved communication and citizen involvement in the police decision-making process.
- Increased job satisfaction and morale among all employees within the department.

Also with regard to the District of Columbia Metropolitan Police Department, it is pioneering the use of a computer system that is designed to cross-reference information for investigations. Literally hundreds of thousands of reports can be shared among investigators, and reports can be accessed instantly, updated readily, and distributed among those seeking specific pieces of data. This breakthrough of information processing and twenty-four-hour availability will be used by federal agencies in the greater metropolitan District of Columbia and is expected to make crime linkages a very sophisticated procedure for the police department. Other major urban departments can be expected to follow this state-of-the-art management approach to information sharing.

CHAPTER 3

JOBS AT THE STATE LEVEL

Comparatively new, yet frequently the easiest to recognize of the modern enforcement units, may be a state police with full criminal enforcement powers or a highway patrol, which may be limited to enforcing the state's motor vehicle code. Because of their twentieth-century origin, these departments tend to be free of some of the early municipal police traditions and have generally managed to mature into well-organized, well-trained, and highly respected organizations.

Although some had modest beginnings in 1835 (Massachusetts) and in 1865 (Texas Rangers), most authors refer to 1903 in Pennsylvania as the beginning of a true statewide agency possessing full enforcement powers. Connecticut in 1903 had a force similar to that of Massachusetts, Arizona in 1901 had a ranger force similar to that in Texas, and New Mexico established mounted police in 1905. Others followed in rapid succession, and today all states except Hawaii have some enforcement unit whose superintendent or director is appointed by the governor and whose jurisdiction is statewide.

Over half of the highway patrols and state police function as one agency within the state's Department of Public Safety. A lesser number operate as separate agencies whose chief administrators report directly to the governor.

The following charts reporting numbers of sworn and civilian state agency personnel are courtesy of the FBI's *Uniform Crime Report.* Note that employment opportunities exist in state agencies beyond the ones with the state police or highway patrol.

Full-time State Law Enforcement Employees, October 31, 1993
State Police or Highway Patrol

STATE	Number of law enforcement employees				
	Total	Officers		Civilians	
		Male	Female	Male	Female
TOTAL	91,262	57,132	3,579	12,195	18,356
ALABAMA					
Department of Public Safety..............................	1,285	628	11	218	428
Other state agencies...........	190	159	6	4	21
ALASKA					
State Police.......................	535	337	19	48	131
ARIZONA					
Department of Public Safety..............................	1,572	842	52	326	352
Other state agencies...........	32	22		6	4
ARKANSAS					
State Police.......................	677	461	19	69	128
CALIFORNIA					
Highway Patrol..................	8,251	5,246	480	1,012	1,513
Other state agencies...........	934	585	86	132	131
COLORADO					
State Patrol	752	519	18	71	144
Other state agencies...........	214	117	22	27	48
CONNECTICUT					
State Police.......................	1,449	908	56	215	270
DELAWARE					
State Police.......................	667	459	30	72	106
Other state agencies...........	180	136	12	16	16
FLORIDA					
Highway Patrol..................	2,097	1,435	153	179	330
Other state agencies...........	2,606	1,138	106	503	859
GEORGIA					
Department of Public Safety..............................	1,976	818	27	398	733
Other state agencies...........	1,406	850	105	138	313

(continued)

| STATE | Number of law enforcement employees | | | | |
| | Total | Officers | | Civilians | |
		Male	Female	Male	Female
IDAHO					
State Police	224	171	6	8	39
Other state agencies	58	41	4	1	12
ILLINOIS					
State Police	3,331	1,716	161	423	1,031
Other state agencies	249	205	15	9	20
INDIANA					
State Police	1,683	995	45	273	370
IOWA					
Department of Public Safety	807	557	27	95	128
KANSAS					
Highway Patrol	804	538	39	113	114
KENTUCKY					
State Police	1,582	894	20	347	321
Other state agencies	875	664	21	69	121
LOUISIANA					
State Police	1,022	711	8	88	215
MAINE					
State Police	482	330	13	77	62
Other state agencies	128	44	2	36	46
MARYLAND					
State Police	2,232	1,485	120	269	358
Other state agencies	1,209	748	120	191	150
MASSACHUSETTS					
State Police	2,514	2,084	201	123	106
MICHIGAN					
State Police	2,916	1,749	189	469	509
MINNESOTA					
State Patrol	683	460	19	121	83
MISSISSIPPI					
Highway Safety Patrol	691	461	8	59	163

STATE	Number of law enforcement employees				
	Total	*Officers*		*Civilians*	
		Male	*Female*	*Male*	*Female*
MISSOURI					
State Highway Patrol.........	1,880	851	15	565	449
MONTANA					
Highway Patrol..................	246	174	15	20	37
Other state agencies...........	339	244	22	32	41
NEBRASKA					
State Patrol	625	462	20	54	89
NEVADA					
Highway Patrol..................	484	299	22	38	125
NEW HAMPSHIRE					
State Police.......................	341	231	21	34	55
NEW JERSEY					
State Police.......................	3,576	2,545	62	413	556
NEW MEXICO					
State Police.......................	573	415	10	49	99
NEW YORK					
State Police.......................	4,636	3,651	287	244	454
Other state agencies...........	416	310	15	69	22
NORTH CAROLINA					
Highway Patrol..................	1,586	1,237	9	198	142
Other state agencies...........	1,860	1,265	114	178	303
NORTH DAKOTA					
Highway Patrol..................	188	119	2	39	28
OHIO					
State Highway Patrol.........	2,431	1,342	84	462	543
OKLAHOMA					
Department of Public Safety.................................	1,271	711	6	266	288
OREGON					
State Police.......................	1,002	752	39	51	160

(continued)

STATE	Number of law enforcement employees				
	Total	Officers		Civilians	
		Male	Female	Male	Female
PENNSYLVANIA					
State Police	5,160	3,957	143	479	581
Other state agencies	305	233	26	8	38
RHODE ISLAND					
State Police	223	167	13	25	18
SOUTH CAROLINA					
Highway Patrol	1,188	959	20	52	157
Other state agencies	999	705	88	36	170
SOUTH DAKOTA					
Highway Patrol	240	155	2	61	22
TENNESSEE					
Department of Public Safety	1,568	720	22	175	651
TEXAS					
Department of Public Safety	5,594	2,426	65	888	2,215
UTAH					
Highway Patrol	398	350	19	8	21
VERMONT					
State Police	406	259	10	52	85
VIRGINIA					
State Police	2,315	1,646	50	201	418
Other state agencies	1,267	314	29	558	366
WASHINGTON					
State Patrol	1,931	943	40	502	446
WEST VIRGINIA					
State Police	804	478	13	99	214
Other state agencies	116	110	1		5
WISCONSIN					
State Patrol	660	433	62	81	84
Other state agencies	63	37	11	7	8
WYOMING					
Highway Patrol	290	141	2	52	95

Full-time, State Law Enforcement Employees, 1993
Limited Jurisdiction, Specialized, and Regulatory Agencies

STATE	Total employees	Officers Male	Female	Civilians Male	Female
ALABAMA: 309 agencies;					
Population 4,181,000	12,429	7,906	676	1,494	2,353
ALASKA: 36 agencies;					
Population 599,000	1,653	974	69	167	443
ARIZONA: 99 agencies;					
Population 3,927,000	13,461	7,194	683	2,586	2,998
ARKANSAS: 183 agencies;					
Population 2,419,900	5,208	3,180	193	815	1,020
CALIFORNIA: 481 agencies;					
Population 27,959,000	85,750	52,878	5,891	8,940	18,041
COLORADO: 235 agencies;					
Population 3,563,000	11,278	7,334	964	788	2,192
CONNECTICUT: 100 agencies;					
Population 2,786,000	8,862	6,710	455	534	1,163
DELAWARE: 45 agencies;					
Population 693,000	2,622	1,898	157	212	355
DISTRICT OF COLUMBIA: 2 agencies;					
Population 578,000	5,222	3,425	965	283	549
FLORIDA: 357 agencies;					
Population 13,449,000	56,328	29,187	3,519	9,784	13,838
GEORGIA: 603 agencies;					
Population 6,721,000	25,474	16,588	2,314	2,148	4,424
HAWAII: 5 agencies;					
Population 1,172,000	3,384	2,528	175	221	460
IDAHO: 109 agencies;					
Population 1,098,000	2,683	1,828	188	130	537
ILLINOIS: 715 agencies;					
Population 11,643,000	39,058	26,789	3,129	3,179	5,961

(continued)

STATE	Total employees	Officers		Civilians	
		Male	Female	Male	Female
INDIANA: 231 agencies;					
Population 5,546,000	13,404	8,192	627	2,013	2,572
IOWA: 225 agencies;					
Population 2,789,000	6,093	4,209	230	502	1,152
KANSAS: 338 agencies;					
Population 2,466,000	8,092	5,425	458	753	1,456
KENTUCKY: 392 agencies;					
Population 3,743,000	8,938	6,266	588	851	1,233
LOUISIANA: 173 agencies;					
Population 4,293,000	15,901	11,216	2,294	758	1,633
MAINE: 134 agencies;					
Population 1,227,000	2,641	1,900	81	305	355
MARYLAND: 125 agencies;					
Population 4,852,000	16,426	11,336	1,410	1,364	2,316
MASSACHUSETTS: 296 agencies;					
Population 5,890,000	16,915	13,634	853	938	1,490
MICHIGAN: 569 agencies;					
Population 9,438,000	24,905	16,730	1,950	2,417	3,808
MINNESOTA: 250 agencies;					
Population 4,172,000	9,351	6,190	460	1,038	1,663
MISSISSIPPI: 164 agencies;					
Population 2,144,000	5,420	3,531	259	616	1,014
MISSOURI: 288 agencies;					
Population 5,124,000	14,186	9,231	836	1,707	2,412
MONTANA: 98 agencies;					
Population 838,000	2,061	1,278	58	248	477
NEBRASKA: 161 agencies;					
Population 1,599,000	3,982	2,670	220	283	809

STATE	Total employees	Officers		Civilians	
		Male	Female	Male	Female
NEVADA: 32 agencies;					
Population 1,380,000	4,739	2,959	358	279	1,143
NEW HAMPSHIRE: 111 agencies;					
Population 929,000	2,492	1,814	87	160	431
NEW JERSEY: 530 agencies;					
Population 7,603,000	34,059	25,836	1,339	2,255	4,629
NEW MEXICO: 93 agencies;					
Population 1,536,000	4,701	3,045	223	444	989
NEW YORK: 392 agencies;					
Population 16,139,000	65,591	45,394	5,702	4,417	10,078
NORTH CAROLINA: 499 agencies;					
Population 6,935,000	20,942	14,146	1,622	2,087	3,087
NORTH DAKOTA: 99 agencies;					
Population 634,000	1,335	930	65	123	217
OHIO: 491 agencies;					
Population 10,130,000	24,835	16,625	1,530	2,621	4,059
OKLAHOMA: 284 agencies;					
Population 3,176,000	8,916	5,644	420	1,223	1,629
OREGON: 169 agencies;					
Population 2,948,000	6,160	4,282	355	290	1,233
PENNSYLVANIA: 875 agencies;					
Population 9,090,000	25,123	19,790	1,848	1,324	2,161
RHODE ISLAND: 41 agencies;					
Population 994,000	2,739	2,127	103	239	270
SOUTH CAROLINA: 241 agencies;					
Population 3,624,000	9,762	6,874	575	757	1,556

(continued)

STATE	Total employees	Officers		Civilians	
		Male	Female	Male	Female
SOUTH DAKOTA: 80 agencies;					
Population 620,000....................	1,152	781	39	124	208
TENNESSEE: 252 agencies;					
Population 4,705,000.................	14,144	8,816	828	1,759	2,741
TEXAS: 880 agencies;					
Population 18,025,000..............	62,829	35,380	3,542	10,434	13,473
UTAH: 121 agencies;					
Population 1,852,000.................	4,232	3,161	280	157	634
VERMONT: 51 agencies;					
Population 576,000....................	1,144	789	46	98	211
VIRGINIA: 270 agencies;					
Population 6,478,000.................	18,219	12,274	1,258	1,573	3,144
WASHINGTON: 221 agencies;					
Population 5,157,000.................	11,640	7,613	597	1,122	2,308
WEST VIRGINIA: 242 agencies;					
Population 1,514,000.................	3,646	2,492	93	525	536
WISCONSIN: 318 agencies;					
Population 4,897,000.................	14,321	9,933	1,120	1,016	2,252
WYOMING: 66 agencies;					
Population 469,000....................	1,678	1,051	58	158	411

STATE POLICE AND HIGHWAY PATROL

All state patrol agencies require high school graduation (or the equivalent) and several now require some amount of college. In Florida, for example, the highway patrol, since 1994, has encouraged applicants to possess two years of college (60 credits), and gives priority hiring status to those with college backgrounds. Likewise, for several years now, some other states, reaching from Delaware to Texas to Washington, have all given hiring preferences to job candidates with two years of higher education.

With regard to minimum age, there has been a downward trend in the last few years, and approximately one-third of the organizations permit entrance at less than twenty-one years of age. Another previous requirement experiencing a decline is height, with most of the departments reporting that they no longer have a height minimum. Specific details as to physical requirements can be obtained from the headquarters unit in your state capital. In general, however, there is little difference from those characteristics described for entry into local police service. In other words, candidates may expect qualifying written examinations administered through a civil service, or state merit system. Also, one can expect a rigorous, comprehensive physical exam to determine stamina, agility, general suitability to the tasks, and that eyesight and hearing are at acceptable standards. All state agencies with sworn officers to be hired will conduct interviews, and most will require psychological testing and polygraph clearance. Likewise, a very thorough and exhaustive background investigation can be anticipated.

Since both the state police and the highway patrol are quasi-military units, the rank system begins with private, and, after achieving satisfactory proficiency ratings and service, the trooper can advance to private first class. Then, through written and oral examinations and maintaining satisfactory proficiency ratings, the trooper can be promoted from corporal through sergeant and into the ranks of lieutenant, captain, and so on. In almost all departments, the superintendent carries the rank of colonel.

The highway patrol enforces the Motor Vehicle Code and works primarily on state highways, interstate systems, and roads in the unincorporated areas of the counties. In some states, greater enforcement powers are being delegated to the highway patrol as it becomes evident that the use of the automobile is associated with crime. The state police officer, in contrast to the highway patrol, does have full police powers throughout the state, although in practice more of the work is in the unincorporated community. In terms of the daily routine, however, the state police officer also spends considerable time enforcing the Motor Vehicle Code on the highways. Either the highway patrol or the state police can legally function where city or town police exist, but they usually do so only at the request of city officials or upon order from the governor. Such requests and orders are most likely to occur during such emergency situations as natural disasters, civil disorders, or excessive criminal activities beyond the capability of the local agency.

In general, whether state officers are employed by the highway patrol or the state police, their training is lengthy and thorough. Recruits in these departments commonly undergo four to six months' training at recruit academies—during which time they receive intensive firearms and physical training, as well as instruction relating to their many enforcement responsibilities.* The classroom training is always supplemented with field experience so the new trooper has considerable opportunity to practice what has been studied in the academy.** Some of the most rigorous law enforcement training is that experienced by the trooper. The trooper's day is very similar to that of an army recruit; it begins early in the morning with physical training and continues into the evening with study and maintenance of equipment. In addition to classroom hours studying criminal law, traffic ordinances, accident investigation, and community relations, the recruit must practice pursuit driving, first aid, the use of weapons, and completing detailed reports.

As assignments of state police officers to urban settings increase, there has been a major commitment to training in human relations, citizen relationships, and interpersonal skills. In some states recent attempts to reduce driving under the influence of alcohol and/or drugs have expanded the duties of the trooper far beyond routine patrol and accident investigation. State officers may be called upon to assist and support the local police, with local traffic control and enforcement or through actual back-up actions with full enforcement powers.

Although duty in the state organization may involve some transfers and reassignment to other sections of that state, there is much to be said for the opportunities in either state police or highway patrol units. Troopers nearly always patrol alone and, therefore, must possess versatility and a capacity for taking full responsibility in a critical situation. They often perform some distance away from their headquarters and

---

*As reported in the *Comparative Data Report* of the International Association of Chiefs of Police, the average number of hours spent by recruits in a training academy is 1,000 hours for highway patrols and also 1,000 hours for state police departments.

**As also reported by the IACP, the average number of hours that recruits spend on the road in supervised field training is 450 hours for highway patrols and 500 hours for the state police.

their superiors. They must be prepared, through temperament and training, to adapt rapidly to a variety of circumstances. A trooper's day may lead from investigating a fatal traffic crash to recovering a stolen automobile or apprehending fleeing holdup suspects. In approximately half the states, the trooper with full police powers may be called upon to handle any crime-related complaint that arises in the unincorporated communities being served. Then, too, at the request of either municipal officials or the governor, the state officer may be called into the incorporated city to reinforce or otherwise aid the local police.

Significant increases in personnel have been authorized at state agencies to meet the greater patrol responsibilities on new expressways and interstate highways. Calls to assist local and suburban police, particularly with specialized functions, also continue to increase.

CIVILIAN POSITIONS

In addition to uniformed officers, there are numerous civilians employed by the state. Almost one-third of the total employees of state police agencies are, in fact, civilians. These include technical personnel in state crime laboratories and employees responsible for motor vehicle registration, driver and licensing examinations, and motor vehicle inspection. A young person interested in such employment should contact the headquarters unit in the state capital for detailed information and specific requirements.

Consider the personnel required to operate the computers and meet the legal requirements associated with auto registrations, licensing, and recording and analyzing accident information. Writers, photographers, clerical help, mathematicians, and technicians of various kinds are needed in many different departments.

OTHER REGULATORY UNITS

Duty at the state level is by no means restricted to the state police or the highway patrol. A number of regulatory, licensing, and protective functions exist that also require competent personnel. Examples of these many agencies are included in a list from the state of California.

This list was chosen because it is perhaps the most inclusive insofar as state responsibility for licensing and regulation goes. All states have these various functions performed in some manner, but they may not be accomplished through specific departments and agencies. A young person interested in a career that includes enforcement responsibilities but has as its main purpose something other than traditional policing would be well advised to consider some of these employment opportunities. For instance, someone particularly interested in outdoor activities and nature might consider a career in a state regulatory agency that protects wildlife or preserves our natural surroundings. Certain state agencies exercise limited policing functions in such widely diversified fields as communications, public health, transportation, and welfare. Again, individuals may select a career that satisfies their interest in the enforcement task, while pursuing another goal that is not limited to policing. An example of this might be conducting investigations for the state fire marshal's office or working at the many inspections performed by state agents—from food and drugs to horse racing and industrial safety.

Salaries for state law enforcement officers are likely, for the most part, to be fairly comparable to those of police counterparts in the region served. Beginning salaries are mostly in the $25,000 to $28,000 range. Some higher maximum salaries for troopers are found in New York and California, which both top $41,000. The highest, at this writing, would appear to be New Jersey in the upper-$40,000 range. Other states where maximum salaries are quite attractive by comparison are Texas, Pennsylvania, and Michigan.

GOVERNMENTAL UNITS POSSESSING POLICE POWER IN THE STATE OF CALIFORNIA

Department of Agriculture
Division of Dairy Industry
  Bureau of Milk Stabilization
Division of Compliance
  Bureau of Livestock Identification
  Bureau of Market Enforcement
  Bureau of Weights and Measures
Division of Plant Industry
  Bureau of Plant Quarantine
  Bureau of Plant Pathology
Division of Animal Industry
  Bureau of Animal Health
  Bureau of Dairy Science
  Bureau of Meat Inspection

  Bureau of Poultry Inspection
Department of Alcoholic Beverage Control

Youth and Adult Corrections Agency
Department of Corrections
  Adult Authority
  Board of Trustees of the California Institution for Women
  Adult Parole Division
Department of Youth Authority

California Disaster Office
Law Enforcement Division

Department of California Highway Patrol

Department of Education
Division of Departmental Administration
California Program for Peace
Officers' Training

Department of Employment
Division of Public Employment
Offices and Benefit Payments

Department of Finance
Building and Grounds Division
California State Police

Department of Industrial Relations
Division of Housing
Division of Industrial Welfare
Industrial Welfare Commission
Division of Industrial Safety
Division of Labor Law Enforcement
Fair Employment Practice Commission

Department of Insurance
Compliance and Legal Division
Policy Complaints Bureau

Department of Investments
Division of Corporations
Division of Real Estate
Division of Savings and Loans

Department of Justice
Division of Criminal Law and Enforcement
Bureau of Criminal Identification
and Investigations
Bureau of Narcotic Enforcement

Department of Mental Hygiene

Department of Motor Vehicles
Division of Registration
Division of Drivers' Licenses
Division of Field Office Operation

Department of Professional and Vocational Standards
Division of Investigation
Board of Accountancy

Board of Architectural Examiners
Athletic Commission
Board of Barber Examiners
Cemetery Board
Board of Chiropractic Examiners
Board of Registration for Civil
and Professional Engineers
Contractors' State License Board
Board of Cosmetology
Board of Dental Examiners
Bureau of Private Investigators
and Adjusters
Board of Dry Cleaners
Board of Funeral Directors and
Embalmers
Board of Furniture and Bedding
Inspection
Board of Guide Dogs for the Blind
Board of Medical Examiners
Board of Nursing Education and
Nurse Registration
Board of Optometry
Board of Pharmacy
Board of Social Work Examiners
Structural Pest Control Board
Board of Examiners in Veterinary
Medicine
Yacht and Ship Brokers' Commission
Board of Vocational Nurse Examiners
Collection Agency Licensing
Bureau
Board of Landscape Architects
The Certified Shorthand
Reporters' Board

Department of Public Health
Bureau of Communicable
Diseases
Bureau of Sanitary Engineering
Bureau of Hospitals
Bureau of Foods and Drugs
Inspection
Division of Laboratories

Resources Agency
Department of Parks and Recreation
Division of Beaches and Parks
Department of Conservation
   Division of Forestry
   Division of Mines and Geology
   Division of Oil and Gas
Department of Fish and Game
   Wildlife Protection Branch
San Francisco Port Authority
Harbor Police

Department of Social Work
State Fire Marshal
Office of Consumer Counsel
Board of Equalization
Department of Business Taxes
State Board of Osteopathic Examiners
California Horse Racing Board
Bureau of Investigations
License Bureau

Of course, it's entirely possible that not all of the above agencies operate in your state; however, it is quite probable that the functions are performed by someone. A wise course of action would be to visit or write the office of the governor, or a state administrator, such as the secretary of state or the office of your local state senator or representative, or state attorney general. Also, other possible sources of guidance and assistance might be the state's Standards and Training Commission or Board in the capital city.

Thus, employment options at the state level are not at all limited; whether the assignment be parks, recreational areas, historical monuments, pollution violations, health hazards, communicable diseases, hazardous environments, fire prevention, wildlife protection, dairy and livestock regulation, insurance fraud, or industrial safety, one thing remains clear: There is job diversity.

The following list will assist the job aspirant in making direct contact with state police and highway patrol headquarters:

Department of Public Safety
   P.O. Box 1511
   500 Dexter Avenue
   Montgomery, AL 36192

Alaska State Troopers
   Department of Public Safety
   5700 E. Tudor Road
   Anchorage, AK 99507

Arizona Highway Patrol
   Department of Public Safety
   2310 N. Twentieth Avenue
   P.O. Box 6638
   Phoenix, AZ 85005

Arkansas State Police
   P.O. Box 5901
   Little Rock, AK 72215

California Highway Patrol
   2555 First Avenue
   P.O. Box 942898
   Sacramento, CA 94298

California State Police
   815 S Street
   Sacramento, CA 95814

Colorado State Patrol
   700 Kipling Street
   Denver, CO 80215

Connecticut State Police
100 Washington Street
Hartford, CT 06106

Delaware State Police
P.O. Box 430
Dover, DE 19903

Florida Highway Patrol
Neil Kirkman Building
Tallahassee, FL 32399

Georgia Department of Public
Safety
P.O. Box 1456
Atlanta, GA 30371

Department of Attorney General
State Capitol Building
Honolulu, HI 96813

Idaho State Police
P.O. Box 700
Meridian, ID 83680

Illinois State Police
P.O. Box 19461
Springfield, IL 62794

Indiana State Police
State Office Building
100 N. Senate Avenue
Indianapolis, IN 46204

Iowa Department of Public Safety
Wallace State Office Building
Des Moines, IA 50319

Kansas Highway Patrol
122 SW Seventh Street
Topeka, KS 66603

Department of Public Safety
State Police Division
7901 Independence Boulevard
P.O. Box 66614
Baton Rouge, LA 70896

Division of State Police
Department of Public Safety
State Office Building
Frankfort, KY 40601

Maine State Police
36 Hospital Street
Augusta, ME 04330

Maryland State Police
1201 Reistertown Road
Pikesville, MD 21208

Massachusetts State Police
470 Worcester Road
Framingham, MA 01701

Michigan State Police
714 South Harrison Road
East Lansing, MI 48823

Minnesota State Patrol
444 Cedar Street
St. Paul, MN 55101

Mississippi Highway Patrol
Public Safety Department
P.O. Box 958
Jackson, MS 39205

Missouri State Highway Patrol
P.O. Box 568
Jefferson City, MO 65102

Montana Highway Patrol
303 Roberts Street North
Helena, MT 59620

Nebraska State Patrol
P.O. Box 94907
Lincoln, NE 68509

Nevada State Highway Patrol
555 Wright Way
Carson City, NV 89711

Department of Public Safety
James H. Hayes Building
Hazen Drive
Concord, NH 03305

New Jersey State Police
P.O. Box 7068
West Trenton, NJ 08625

New Mexico State Police
P.O. Box 1628
Santa Fe, NM 87504

Division of State Police
State Campus Building 22
Albany, NY 12226

North Carolina State Highway
Patrol
3318 Garner Road
P.O. Box 27687
Raleigh, NC 27611

North Dakota Highway Patrol
State Capitol
600 East Boulevard Avenue
Bismarck, ND 58505

State Highway Patrol
660 East Main Street
Columbus, OH 43205

Oklahoma Department of Public
Safety
P.O. Box 11415
Oklahoma City, OK 73136

Oregon State Police
400 Public Service Building
Salem, OR 97310

Pennsylvania State Police
1800 Elmerton Avenue
Harrisburg, PA 17110

Rhode Island State Police
311 Danielson Pike
P.O. Box 185
North Scituate, RI 02857

State Highway Patrol
5400 Broad River Road
P.O. Drawer 191
Columbia, SC 29210

South Dakota Highway Patrol
500 E. Capitol Avenue
Highway Office Building
Pierre, SD 57501

Tennessee Department of
Public Safety
1150 Foster Avenue
Nashville, TN 37249

Texas Rangers
Department of Public Safety
Box 4087
North Austin Station
Austin, TX 78773

Utah Highway Patrol
4501 South 2700 West
Salt Lake City, UT 84119

Department of Public Safety
103 South Main Street
State Complex
Waterbury, VT 05671

Department of State Police
P.O. Box 27472
Richmond, VA 23261

Washington State Patrol
Headquarters
General Administration
Building
P.O. Box 42601
Olympia, WA 98504

West Virginia State Police
725 Jefferson Road
South Charleston, WV 25309

Wisconsin State Patrol
P.O. Box 7912
Madison, WI 53707

Highway Patrol
Wyoming Highway Department
P.O. Box 1708
Cheyenne, WY 82003

CHAPTER 4

MILITARY AND FEDERAL SERVICES

MILITARY

Opportunities for young people exist in the military services, and it is not unusual to find civilian police personnel who attribute their initial interest in law enforcement to experience gained while serving in the military police, air police, shore patrol, or a military investigative unit.

The Uniform Code of Military Justice is enforced by the military police, and no one should overlook the opportunity to gain this experience. There are ample opportunities for study at specialized schools, patrol and investigative work, promotion through the military ranks, worldwide assignments, and entrance can be accomplished well ahead of the age of twenty-one.

The military gives young people valuable training and the opportunity to learn about law enforcement; it often helps them decide about a career in the field. Some use the military experience as their departure point into civilian policing; others remain for an entire career with the military. The military police are found wherever troops are stationed, and their duties resemble those of local level law officers. They operate on military bases, patrol areas where the military are located, and are generally limited in their jurisdiction to military personnel, or persons involved in illegal activities aimed toward military personnel.

In addition to the military police (MPs), the Department of the Navy has opportunities in its Naval Investigative Service. Likewise, the U.S. Air Force has its Security Police, primarily in uniform with duties similar to those of the military police. There is also an investigative branch termed Office of Special Investigations.

Let's take a brief look at one of these units. The Naval Investigative Service is largely civilian and has some 1,200 special agents worldwide. It is responsible for conducting criminal investigations and counterintelligence operations for both the Navy and the Marine Corps. Its broad spectrum of investigation includes sting operations, undercover drug cases, counterintelligence, dignitary protection, antiterrorism, and contracting and procurement frauds. The Army's Criminal Investigation Division and the Air Force's Office of Special Investigations are similar in responsibilities.

Requirements for all these special agents are similar in terms of college background, careful screening, and sophisticated training in multifaceted subjects.

Since one may join the armed services well ahead of the age when many local or federal organizations will hire, there are some important reasons, in terms of experience and training, for considering the military. Wise police administrators and government bureau chiefs welcome candidates with military experience because such applicants have already attained a sense of maturity and responsibility.

FEDERAL AGENCIES

All federal agencies have specific violation categories in which their jurisdiction lies, and this section lists the official responsibilities and duties of each organization. Because of the many diverse opportunities available throughout the federal government, it would be advisable to obtain detailed qualifications directly from the unit in which one is interested. We have included addresses to help interested people obtain career brochures. Many federal agencies exert considerable effort on recruitment and respond well to job inquiries.

Most, but not all, federal agencies require a bachelor's degree for entrance, and all expect it of those who aspire to promotion. Some federal agencies are more investigative than enforcement oriented and, therefore, may demand a variety of skills, such as legal training or tax knowledge. The Drug Enforcement Administration needs persons trained in pharmacy, while the border patrol requires persons who speak Spanish fluently. Also, many federal officers find that they spend a great deal of time on a particular case or series of cases. Customs agents might spend a long time investigating a smuggling incident; the Internal Revenue Service agent with accounting skills often devotes many hours to verifying failures to pay proper taxes; the Secret Service cannot relax for one moment its watchful protection of the president and vice-president; and the FBI agent may need months to solve a violation involving our national security.

Because their numbers are comparatively small and their salaries and prestige relatively great, federal agents possess high personal qualifications and must survive intensive background investigations. Of the large numbers of applicants for federal work, only the best qualified are selected. All federal officers must be patient, determined, capable of working long hours, willing to travel on a moment's notice, and independent enough to work alone for prolonged periods. Travel outside of the United States is required in certain departments, and unlike local police officers, the federal agent may devote lengthy periods of time to only a few specialized investigations and make few arrests. The federal role also entails detailed reports and court appearances. Federal agents must be articulate, able to deal with all levels of society, and must always perform as symbolic representatives of American justice. Since 1983 the federal government has covered all employees under social security. A twenty-year retirement in most federal agencies, with pension dependent upon salary attained, makes early departure from government service possible. Many take advantage of this retirement program, thereby creating continual vacancies in federal units. In recent years, increasing requests for more federal assistance have increased the budgets of these organizations. As population expands, demand for aid increases, and criminal mobility continues, it can be safely predicted that the United States government will require large numbers of well-qualified and dedicated young persons to fill these important law enforcement positions.

The official description and specific duties of each federal agency appear in the *Organization Manual*. Educational requirements for most federal agencies include a bachelor's degree. A discussion of salary, taken from the current GS scale, appears in Chapter 5. Most law enforcement jobs are at the GS 7, 9, or 10 entrance level.

There is no particular magic to entering federal service. The applicant *must* apply directly to the agency. (See addresses later in this chapter.)

Upon submission of the application, successful completion of the Federal Service Entrance Examination is required. Certain agencies may require tests for memory and retention in addition to the general federal entrance exam. All agencies will require medical data, character and background investigations, and reference checks. All federal enforcement agencies have their own basic training programs, lasting up to six months. These are designed to equip the new agent with skills needed in the field. Much of the course content relates to federal statutes and various investigative procedures.

An important feature of federal enforcement is the continuing in-service training that officers and agents receive. This is practiced most regularly and effectively at the federal level, although it is desirable throughout law enforcement. Since most agencies have divided the country into field service offices, the prospective federal agent must also recognize that travel is a necessary part of the job. On the other hand, an attraction to federal service is the twenty-year retirement plan, with a lifelong pension amounting to a percentage of one's highest salary. This plan enables federal employees to complete their careers while still relatively young, then pursue different employment. A number of college criminal justice professors and local police chiefs are retired from the federal service.

TYPICAL ASSIGNMENTS

Let us review the particular assignments one could expect to have at each of the major federal investigative departments, citing only those duties that are truly enforcement oriented. We will not discuss the many other jobs in those departments that have to do with planning, communications, training, maintenance, records, data, as well as information distribution.

The positions described in this chapter all require an ability to recognize and develop evidence for presentation to U.S. attorneys, to meet and confer with persons engaged in many kinds of activities, to testify effectively in a court of law, to prepare detailed written reports, to operate a motor vehicle, to be proficient in the use of firearms and self-defense, and to exercise continual good judgment, resourcefulness, and initiative.

The *U.S. Postal Service,* formerly the Post Office Department, was established independently in 1970. *Postal inspectors* investigate losses and thefts of the mail or property owned by the post office. In addition, investigators and security force personnel protect postal buildings and installations. There are 3,500 officers employed by the Postal Service, most of whom are classified as criminal investigators; some others provide security for the Postal Service and all its facilities and assets.

There are some eighty-five postal-related laws dealing with such situations as mail box thefts, robberies of postal authorities, embezzlements, frauds using the mails, and post office burglaries. There are also attempts to sell items by mail, obtain funds through fraudulent schemes, and other such acts that may be violations of postal laws. If anyone uses the mail system illegally, as in transporting firearms, narcotics, obscene materials, or incendiary devices, they are likewise the subject of investigation and prosecution by postal inspectors. As is the case with many other federal agents, a very modern crime laboratory is available to support complex investigations.

Several major agencies, employing a total of some 25,000 criminal investigators, operate within the United States Department of Justice. Probably best known is the *Federal Bureau of Investigation,* and agents of this unit are responsible for the enforcement of an extensive variety of statutes. The FBI agent may be assigned to national security matters, rights violations, interstate transportation offenses, and the security of both property and personnel of the federal government. Also within the jurisdiction of the FBI are numerous federal acts that pertain to specific offenses, such as bank robbery, kidnapping, and extortion.

Some 200 different types of cases fall within the jurisdiction of the FBI. Certain offenses are complicated and involve "white-collar" crimes such as embezzlements in banks or organized crime activities. From espionage to terrorism, the FBI agent evaluates many different types of information before presenting it to the Department of Justice for prosecution. Most agents are assigned to one of the fifty-nine divisional offices, although some work at the headquarters in Washington and others in resident agencies around the country. In 1993 there were 10,075 FBI agents, a significant increase over recent years, and 1,000 of those special agents were women.

The FBI operates one of the most outstanding crime laboratories in the world, and all types of examinations may be conducted to assist the agents in the field, or to support investigations by local authorities.

The *Immigration and Naturalization Service,* another part of the Department of Justice, administers our nation's immigration and naturalization laws and is responsible for investigations concerning aliens. Its uniformed agents, referred to as the *border patrol,* are on continuous duty guarding all U.S. points of entry.

The border patrol is highly mobile, uniformed, and its primary duty is to detect and prevent illegal entry into the United States. Agents patrol designated areas and also inspect commercial carriers, terminals, and traffic check points to stop those who attempt to enter the country without proper clearance. The border patrol also has responsibility for deportation actions.

INS investigators, unlike the border patrol, review applications for visas, determine whether aliens may enter or remain in the country, and gather all information for the administrative hearings and criminal prosecution of immigration law violations. At this writing, and always subject to new congressional priorities, the Immigration and Naturalization Service has some 10,000 employed in its various functions. Approximately 4,000 are assigned to border patrol; 4,500 assigned to criminal investigations and enforcement; 1,100 are detention and deportation officers; and most of the inspectors are in port of entry states.

The U.S. Marshals Service provides a general enforcement service, from witness protection to asset forfeiture programs. These officers tend to have prior enforcement experience and fill varied types of assignments, often low-key, and not well known by the general public. Recent legislation granted the Marshals Service authority to enter into contracts and collect fees for operating expenses related to security protection and serving civil process orders of the courts. The same legislation enables the Marshals Service to become involved in jail assistance in exchange for the housing of federal prisoners.

U.S. marshals execute and enforce commands of federal courts, process federal prisoners, seize property under court order, and protect federal judges, witnesses, and juries. The Marshals Service is the oldest federal law enforcement agency and was established during the period of the "Old West." Their major duties are similar to the original ones: attending to the federal courts and executing orders of the United States government. Deputy U.S. marshals are assigned special duties as the needs arise, but basically they still serve both civil and criminal processes of the courts. They serve federal warrants, move and protect federal prisoners and other trial participants, seize property under federal court orders, collect federal funds, and protect facilities. The role of the deputy marshal has always been vital in the area of civil disturbances, and in 1971 a special operations group was established to provide immediate federal response to civil situations. In recent years the deputy marshals also have provided protection for witnesses under the Organized Crime Acts, for missiles being transported, and for airline passengers in conjunction with aircraft hijacking. There are more than 2,200 such persons with U.S. marshal sworn authority.

The *Drug Enforcement Administration,* previously called the Bureau of Narcotics and Dangerous Drugs, is primarily responsible for enforcing laws concerning all narcotic drugs. It also controls the registration provisions of federal drug laws, combats illicit narcotics traffic, and regulates distribution of dangerous drugs. This unit has critical responsibility for determining the quantities of narcotics permissible in the country for medical purposes. In recent years, a sizeable increase in positions has occurred within this federal agency. Over three thousand DEA agents operate in the United States and in more than forty foreign countries.

It is DEA's goal to eliminate illegal sources of drug supply and distribution. Many of these sources are overseas, thus necessitating a variety of strategies involving foreign countries. Drug suppression and interdiction of drug trafficking have become high priorities with the federal government in recent years, and the DEA has the primary role in assisting local agencies.

The DEA agent, often a former police or military officer, has one of the most difficult and dangerous of all federal agent employments. All DEA agents are college graduates, and about 10 percent are women. Screening for this position can take a long time, and the DEA agent's training is initially thirteen weeks. In one recent year, the DEA seized more than $500 million in drug assets including houses, cars, boats, stocks, and businesses. At one time or another, agents will work undercover, and their duties can take them throughout the world. Despite the physical demands and the risks, there are a hundred applicants for every spot in the DEA training academy.

Another large number of federal criminal investigators (20,000) is employed within the agencies of the *U.S. Department of the Treasury.* One of these agencies is the *Customs Service,* which regulates the importation of goods into the country. The Customs Service is especially concerned with smuggling activities that may occur in our ports of entry. This bureau has many responsibilities pertaining to goods being shipped into or from this country. *Customs agents* find their daily duties varying from examining an incoming traveler's luggage to registering the weight of an incoming vessel. Customs Service enforces some 400 revenue and navigational laws and regulations for the federal government; this organization ensures that revenue is paid for incoming goods and prevents prohibited goods from entering or leaving the country. Their priorities include not only the protection of the revenue system, but the health and safety of our citizens. There are several different job levels within the Customs Service including special agents, customs officers, import specialists, and customs inspectors. Quite naturally, these personnel work closely with the DEA, INS, and FBI in dealing with baggage, merchandise, cargo, and other potential locations of tax abuse. Customs Service enforcement personnel number more than 10,000.

Also under the Treasury Department is the *Internal Revenue Service.* In general, IRS *agents'* assignments encompass the U.S. tax revenue system. Agents of this organization, many of whom are professional accountants, perform a variety of duties. They examine taxpayers' records to determine tax liabilities and investigate cases involving tax fraud or evasion of tax payments (such as those pertaining to business or gambling).

Within the Treasury Department are special investigators of the *Alcohol, Tobacco, and Firearms Bureau.* They enforce federal laws governing the manufacture, sale, distribution, and possession of firearms and explosives, alcohol, and tobacco products. Agents of this division regulate and maintain records on the legal taxable production of alcoholic beverages and have authority to apprehend those engaged in illegal activities relating to alcoholic beverages. ATF agents direct much of their effort against terrorist groups, organized crime, and those involved in bombing incidents. Perhaps best known for their work in illicit distillery investigations, the ATF also is empowered to seize and destroy illegal production and distribution networks, and to reduce the smuggling of contraband cigarettes and other untaxed tobacco products. Some 2,000 agents bear the responsibility for the criminal usage of firearms, explosives, and the taxes cited above.

The *Secret Service* has a twofold responsibility: protecting the president and vice-president of the United States, along with their families, and protecting the coins and securities of the government by enforcing laws pertaining to counterfeiting. With over 2,200 agents, the Secret Service also protects the White House, the Treasury Building, and its Foreign Missions Branch and foreign embassies.

Prior to 1978, the Secret Service, which dates back to 1922, operated the White House Police Force; this later became the Executive Protection Service and now is known as the Uniformed Division. Under their officers' continuous protection are the Executive Mansion and its grounds; buildings in which White House offices are located; foreign diplomatic missions and residences, in certain cases; and the official residence of the vice-president.

For the most part the counterfeiting investigations conducted by the U.S. secret service special agent involve stolen checks, bonds, and securities. Forgery of any currency or of signatures in order to cash any governmental obligation such as a check, is the exclusive jurisdiction of this agency. They enjoy an extremely high rate of success in their prosecutions. A relatively recent assignment for the Secret Service will be computer fraud as it affects government securities.

Federal protective officers are under the control of the *General Services Administration;* they are uniformed and authorized to protect property and life within federally owned and operated buildings and adjacent ground and parking areas. Vulnerable entry points and the like are all monitored or secured to maintain law and order on government property.

There are 1,100 men and women employed to police some forty blocks in the heart of the nation's capital and miles of inside corridors. Referred to in Washington guidebooks as "polite and attentive," this group since 1801 has been known as the U.S. Capitol Police. Like all other police patrol units, they issue citations, search packages, check violations, and ensure visitor security. They are also responsible for the protection of members of Congress, committee hearings, and all events that occur within the Capitol grounds.

The U.S. Office of Personnel Management, formerly known as the U.S. Civil Service Commission, maintains a register or listing of qualified candidates for many of the positions described in this section. Contact must be made with that office to establish the basic qualifications for any particular position and to obtain the proper application forms and other related materials. Plan well ahead in pursuing federal jobs because the turnover is often low, the salary and benefits are significant, and there may well be a time lag between first inquiry, being placed officially on the qualified list, and then being hired.

Should one have an interest in law enforcement and wish to follow up that interest by protecting our environment, one of the newer special agent positions is that with the Criminal Investigation Division of the Environmental Protection Agency. These officers work within a structure of sophisticated science and technology to protect our air, water, and land resources.

Within the federal government, there are many other units with enforcement and supervisory responsibilities, such as the Federal Aviation Administration, Occupational Safety and Health Administration, Mining Enforcement and Safety Administration, Public Health Service, Bureau of Sport Fisheries and Wildlife, and Food and Drug Administration. For example, there are over 7,000 *federal food inspectors,* as well as 2,000 *investigators* employed to check on compliance with civil rights statutes. Even less known to the general public, but still offering attractive career opportunities, are such federal positions as the 1,000 *Office of Federal Investigations staff* working from the Office of Personnel Management (OPM), who conduct personal and record inquiries into backgrounds for federal service applicants, and 150 *Consumer Product Safety Commission investigators.* In addition, the person who enjoys farm and rural life should not overlook the fact that over 8,400 *investigators* work for the *Agriculture Department.* For those interested in game, wildlife, and outdoor recreation, the *Department of the Interior* employs nearly 2,200 *investigators* for its parks and wildlife refuges. In addition the *General Services Administration* employs nearly 3,500 persons to conduct criminal and civil investigations of collusion, bribery, conflicts of interest, thefts from government jurisdictions, and offenses specified in the acts protecting government personnel and procedures. The *National Park Service,* employing more than 2,000 sworn personnel, offers some of the most fascinating and appealing assignments in the federal service. This includes the U.S. Park Police, and their authority reaches throughout the National Park system.

A few others worth specific mention, because of their uniqueness and specialization, are the Tennessee Valley Authority (740 officers); the U.S. Forest Service (730); and the U.S. Fish and Wildlife Service, whose refuge officers and special investigative agents total over 600 personnel.

In addition to the large and well-known federal enforcement organizations, there are many *independent agencies* responsible for highly specialized and technical enforcement. These include the Federal Communications Commission, Federal Maritime Commission, Federal Power Commission, Nuclear Regulatory Commission, Federal Trade Commission, Federal Emergency Management Agency, National Aeronautics & Space Administration, as well as the Interstate Commerce Commission.

Beyond criminal investigative positions in the federal government, there are numerous *intelligence specialists* whose primary duties relate to background clearances and security personnel matters. These include persons employed by the Central Intelligence Agency, National Security Agency, Defense Investigative Service, and special agents of the Department of State and Office of Federal Investigations.

One statistic of interest to young career aspirants is that although the U.S. government employs its enforcement personnel literally throughout the world, the majority are assigned in California, with the next largest numbers in Texas, New York, District of Columbia, and Florida, in that order.

Interested young people are urged to contact these federal agencies directly because all of them have specific career information available.

FOR MORE INFORMATION

Department of Defense

Dept. of the Army
  Pentagon Headquarters
  Washington, DC 20310

Dept. of the Air Force
  Pentagon Headquarters
  Washington, DC 20330

Dept. of the Navy
  Pentagon Headquarters
  Washington, DC 20350

Dept. of Defense
  Inspector General
  400 Army/Navy Drive
  Arlington, VA 22202

Department of Health and Human Services

Public Health Service
  5600 Fishers Lane
  Rockville, MD 20852

Food and Drug Administration
5600 Fishers Lane
Rockville, MD 20852

Department of the Interior
Bureau of Indian Affairs
1951 Constitution Avenue, NW
Washington, DC 20245

National Park Service
Interior Department Bldg.
Washington, DC 20240

Fish and Wildlife Service
1612 K Street, NW
Washington, DC 20240

Department of Justice
Federal Bureau of Investigation
J. Edgar Hoover Building
Tenth Street & Pennsylvania
Avenue, NW
Washington, DC 20535

Federal Bureau of Prisons
320 First Street, NW
Washington, DC 20534

Drug Enforcement
Administration
1110 Eye Street, NW
Washington DC 20537

Immigration & Naturalization
Service
425 Eye Street, NW
Washington, DC 20536

Interpol; (International Criminal
Police Organization)
1405 Eye Street, NW
USNC B
Washington, DC 20530

U.S. Marshals Service
600 Army Navy Drive
Arlington, VA 22202

Department of State
Recruitment & Employment
Division
Bureau of Diplomatic Security
2121 Virginia Avenue, NW
Washington, DC 20522

Department of Agriculture
Office of Inspector General
Fourteenth and Independence
Avenue, SW
Washington, DC 20250

Department of Labor
200 Constitution Avenue, NW
Washington, DC 20210

U.S. Department of Commerce
Office of the Inspector General
Washington, DC 20230

U.S. Coast Guard
Law Enforcement & Defense
Operations
2100 Second Street SW
Washington, DC 20593

U.S. Park Police
1100 Ohio Drive SW
Washington, DC 20242

Department of the Treasury
Bureau of Alcohol, Tobacco, &
Firearms
650 Massachusetts Avenue, NW
Washington, DC 20001

U.S. Customs Service
1301 Constitution Avenue, NW
Washington, DC 20229

Internal Revenue Service
1111 Constitution Avenue, NW
Washington, DC 20224

U.S. Secret Service
1800 G Street, NW
Washington, DC 20223

Department of Transportation
U.S. Coast Guard
2100 Second Street, SW
Washington, DC 20590

General Services Administration
General Services Administration
Office of Personnel
Eighteenth & F Streets, NW
Washington, DC 20405

U.S. Postal Service
  475 L'Enfant Plaza West
  Inspection Services Office
  Washington, DC 20260

United States Congress
  Capitol Police
  U.S. Capitol Bldg.
  Washington, DC 20510
  or
  119 D Street, NE
  Washington, DC 20510

Additional Agencies

Agency of International
  Development
  U.S. Dept. of State
  2201 C Street, NW
  Washington, DC 20520

Environmental Protection Agency
  401 M Street, SW
  Washington, DC 20460

Department of Housing &
  Urban Development
  Inspector General's Office
  451 Seventh Street, SW
  Washington, DC 20410

Inspector General
  Government Printing Office
  N. Capitol & H Streets, NW
  Washington, DC 20401

Department of Energy
  Security Branch
  1000 Independence Avenue, SW
  Washington, DC 20585

Federal Emergency Management
  Agency
  500 C Street, SW
  Washington, DC 20472

Federal Protective Services
  Eighteenth & F Streets, NW
  Washington, DC 20405

Park Police
  1100 Ohio Drive, SW
  Washington, DC 20242

Safety & Security Inspections Office
  Department of Transportation
  400 Seventh Street, SW
  Washington, DC 20590

National Highway Traffic Safety
  Administration
  400 Seventh Street, NW
  Washington, DC 20590

Federal Aviation Administration
  800 Independence Avenue, SW
  Washington, DC 20591

For additional assistance and information contact the Office of Personnel Management, 1900 E Street, Washington, DC 20415, or Division of Federal Investigations, Personnel Management Office, P.O. Box 7544, Washington, DC 20044–7544.

There are regional offices of the Office of Personnel Management. One might best be guided by seeking advice and information, as well as application forms, from an office closest to home.

75 Spring Street, SW
  Atlanta, GA 30303

Federal Building
  230 Dearborn Street
  Chicago, IL 60604

211 Main Street
  San Francisco, CA 94105

Federal Building
  600 Arch Street
  Philadelphia, PA 19106

1100 Commerce Street
  Dallas, TX 75242

CHAPTER 5

EMPLOYMENT AND COMPENSATION

Criminal and civil justice is a personnel-intensive activity. In 1993 state and local governments spent 81 percent of their law enforcement budgets on police salaries. Salaries make up a lower proportion of spending for corrections (59 percent), primarily because of the costs of building and maintaining institutions. Estimates about the cost of crime to government reached $80 *billion* in 1993. These are actual expenditures, not losses, and of that amount, about $40 *billion* was at the local level of government. Another way of measuring expenditures is to observe that 48 cents of every justice dollar is spent for police (See chart, Criminal Justice System Costs, 1990, at the end of this chapter.)

The salary progress that law enforcement has achieved in recent years relates to several factors: the state standardization of training, the awarding of certification, educational progress toward individual professional stature, and a general increase in public support and community recognition of the duties of police officers. Starting and maximum salaries are both quite competitive with the salaries offered by other employers who seek personnel of the same age, educational level, and experience.

The average salary for police officers has increased at least fifty percent in the last decade, and large numbers of police patrol officers now work in cities where the maximum salary is over $30,000, and may even reach $40,000 with overtime. In the late 1970s, average starting salaries were slightly above $12,000. By the early 1980s, those same city averages were up to nearly $15,000. In 1993, according to the International City Managers' Association, the starting patrol officer salary reached $20,700. This national average figure includes many smaller towns and less populated communities. In Florida the statewide average initial salary is now $22,200. However, cities such as Hollywood and Davie, Florida, are starting officers at nearly $31,000.

Let us review some starting salaries as they were reported by selected communities in 1990. San Jose, California, advertised for beginning officers at $35,000, with increases going to nearly $45,000 after several years. Historically, California has led the nation in police salaries. One of the best known departments, the City of Los Angeles, advertises for police to start at $33,000. This is for someone at age twenty-one with a high school diploma. For successful applicants with college preparation, the salary begins at $35,400. Salaries for Los Angeles patrol officers with experience can reach $42,000.

It should be noted, too, that cities such as San Jose, and Bellevue, Washington, require that their police candidates have higher educational achievements, up to and including a two-year college degree. The Metro-Dade (Florida) County Police Department starts an officer at $27,000 upon academy completion, and the top of their officer salary scale is now reaching $36,000. In Texas, in cities such as Houston and Dallas, there are competitive salaries for young people as they approach age twenty-one. The New York City Police Department reports a starting salary of over $30,000 as well. The City of Miami, Florida, now begins its officers at $29,000 with annual increases up to nearly $39,000. Next door, in Miami Beach, the police starting salary is $29,000 also, and the maximum salary is over $36,000. Also in Florida, the cities of Coral Gables, Gainesville, and Tallahassee all require two years of college to enter their police departments. Coral Gables pays $29,000 to start.

Let us look at the Midwest where the Kettering, Ohio, police begin their officers at $28,000 per year. This agency requires either prior experience or two years of college. Also in the Midwest, Madison, Wisconsin, advertises that it is a police department where young people would want to work. Its ad states that the department is committed to employee involvement, problem solving, and community oriented policing. It boasts the type of organization where individuals can and do make a difference. Its starting salary is about $28,000.

To illustrate the variations within a rather close geographical region, consider that the capital city of Harrisburg, Pennsylvania, starts officers at $22,000 and nearby Northern York Regional Police begins at $21,000. In the same area, a Pennsylvania state trooper begins at

$24,000. The top of the scale for a trooper is $36,000, in Harrisburg officers make up to $29,000, and in York Regional the top scale for an officer is $35,000.

As we have been indicating, salaries do vary: sometimes because of the type of agency and its size; sometimes because of geographic differences that reflect themselves in regional industrial competition; and sometimes due only to historical reasons and how public employment and local government generally has fared in that region over the course of time.

It is wise to make careful comparisons that reach beyond merely the basic entrance salary figure. How many pay steps are there before reaching the top of the officer scale? What has been that organization's history with regard to pay increases and increments? What financial reward does promotion bring, and is it significantly higher than the rates paid to patrol officer rank?

It has been observed for many years now that police officers often enjoy higher salaries than those in other public service careers and other categories of public employment. These other endeavors include social workers, nurses, public school teachers, and journalists. These occupations also require formal education and specialized training. Furthermore the evidence continues to mount that policing is a career field on the move upward: income levels have been steadily rising, police officers receive overtime for extra duty, special hazard pay is available for certain assignments, and many locales now award incentive pay for educational and training attainments. Anyone seriously considering employment in law enforcement should seek out those progressive agencies that provide monies for educational attainment.

Some estimate that more than half of all cities offer incentives or salary increases for higher education or specialized training. A decade ago only 37 percent of the departments reported such incentive programs. A 1988 study by the Police Executive Research Forum in Washington, DC reported that nearly 14 percent of agencies surveyed required some higher education for police entrance. A typical salary incentive plan, whether state supported or local, may add an additional fifty dollars per month for an associate degree and one hundred dollars per month for the bachelor's degree.

A creative and substantial pay plan for educational attainment is found in the City of St. Louis, Missouri, where a starting police patrol officer is scheduled at $27,400 with an immediate increase to $30,000 with a bachelor's degree. That same officer, after five years of service, could expect to receive a salary of $38,000. Salt Lake City pays new officers $26,000, with increases to $36,800 for merit.

In nearby Kansas City, Missouri, the officer begins with a salary of $25,300, plus a possible educational incentive, and can reach a very substantial top salary of approximately $45,000. A similar pay scale prevails for the County Police Department in St. Louis.

Students are well advised to seek out agencies where incentive pay is available for higher education, not merely for the additional salary it offers, but more importantly because it suggests a commitment to professional stature and top quality that is most important in seeking one's career affiliation. A good rule of thumb, for career guidance, is to look at the basic salary for academy study and immediately upon entrance, the range for entry positions, and what the top level command jobs pay. Also, see if they provide educational incentives.

Salary variations are important to anyone seeking a career, and it is always advisable to obtain the latest salary figures from the specific department of interest. This information is easy to obtain and will usually be quoted in any job vacancy notice, even in local newspapers and ads. With contract negotiations occurring in many jurisdictions, and with the general fiscal priorities that police protection enjoys, a salary quoted in print may be out of date by the time the applicant is sworn into the position.

All recruiting notices should outline salary and fringe benefits, as well as required work week, paid holidays, policy for leaves and sick benefits, life insurance, and so forth. It must be emphasized that because these matters are constantly improving, no figures should be regarded as definitive unless they are from the agency's own official notice. And again, extra pay may be available for hazardous duty with motorcycles, helicopters, patrol boats, or as a dog handler, to say nothing of overtime.

Officers may receive additional percentages for midnight shift duty or for teaching in the academy during off-duty hours. Of course, promotion to higher rank brings additional income. In most jurisdictions, assignment to the detective or investigative unit adds additional salary also.

It would be difficult in a national publication to discuss salaries above those at the entry level. It can be assumed that moving up the rank structure brings monetary increases, in addition to the normal pay raises based on seniority. One method of gaining insight into the career potential for remuneration is to look at what the top jobs pay. Again, they vary widely. Some sheriffs who serve as constitutional officers, some state police superintendents who serve as members of the governor's cabinet, and some city chiefs of police earn in the range of $80,000 to $100,000. Salem, Oregon, is right at $80,000 for top positions.

To cite a few illustrations of top level command salaries, note that the chief of police in San Diego, California, earns $87,000. His counterpart in Rockville, Maryland, is listed at $68,000. The chief of police for Minneapolis, Minnesota, is reportedly paid $67,000. In Washington, DC, the chief's salary is slightly over $75,000. Cities such as New York, Los Angeles, and Chicago all report paying their police chiefs in the $120,000 range. The County of St. Louis, Missouri, offers $87,000. Chiefs of police have a wide salary range in many of America's cities. Size of agency has much to do with that range. A typical salary for a major police executive would most likely fall in the category where one finds the St. Louis, Missouri, City Department, i.e., $75,000. If the commissioner of the Pennsylvania State Police is typical, the salary figure of $80,000 also prevails. A national advertisement for chief of police in Richmond, Virginia, sets top pay for that position at $77,662. Some other recent listings show chief ranges from $63,000 in Springfield, Missouri, to $76,000 in Claremont, California, to $75,000 in Kansas City, Kansas, to $99,000 in Kansas City, Missouri. In a police-related position, where the job appointee is on leave from his sworn position, the state of Florida drug coordinator pays $80,000. There are also relatively new positions, such as directors of state training commissions, which pay in the range of $50,000 to $60,000. Reviewing a recent issue of the *Police Chief* magazine, one finds chiefs of police advertisements listing salaries from the mid-$50,000 to mid-$60,000 range; $53,774; $72,000; and for a modest-sized community, $38,000. Therefore, the range is quite substantial for the top executives in the field, and the major factor continues to be the size of the community and the overall budgetary responsibilities.

Clearly, not all careerists can expect to achieve the position of chief of police in their particular locale, and salaries such as commissioner in New York City or chief in Los Angeles may not be typical anywhere else. But there are many high-level officers who enjoy comparatively high salaries. The titles of *deputy chief, assistant chief, deputy commissioner,* along with *lieutenant colonels* and *majors,* all attain salaries only slightly less than that of the top administrator, and these are all realistic goals for the serious career-minded professional.

Although there may be only one chief, sheriff, or director, there may be a team of a half-dozen top command personnel supporting policy decisions. These officials, usually the products of that organization, will be paid salaries well within reach of the chief's. Again, to use our illustration of the Metro Dade Police Department in Florida, the current range for a division chief, of which there are several, is $85,000 to $90,000.

FRINGE BENEFITS

In addition to competitive salaries, enforcement agencies traditionally have offered many fringe benefits comparable to or exceeding those of private industry. For many years, law enforcement has advertised and prided itself on the retirement system it made available to officers. Likewise, sick and injury leave provisions have been attractive. Generally speaking, after twenty years of service, officers can retire with a specific percentage of their highest salary. Most likely, this can be done at age fifty or fifty-five. Should the employee remain with the agency for twenty-five or more years, the percentage of salary paid for retirement increases accordingly. Police officers often retire at age fifty-five while those in business or industry have another ten years to work before the usual retirement age of sixty-five.

Group health and life insurance programs are universal in law enforcement work. Vacation, holiday, and other leave arrangements are considered routine policies and will not vary greatly among communities. Of course, disability insurance exists in the event an officer is injured in the line of duty.

Local level law enforcement provides relatively good job security, most likely through a form of civil service or local merit system. Then, too, many more communities now have unions or police employee associations to afford further job protection.

Again, as with salaries and upward mobility, job applicants should ask questions about hospitalization insurance, dental and vision plans, leaves for maternity where applicable, and other benefits. Such an item as overtime provisions can be very important when making salary comparisons. Likewise, off-duty approved employment is often available and encouraged. Some communities have various arrangements to encourage and reward high education. The job seeker is well advised to inquire about tuition payment plans, tuition reimbursements, and any salary incentives for educational attainments.

Typically, most police agencies operated a work schedule that reflected three eight-hour shifts, often rotating personnel every week or two. Drawbacks to the traditional work schedules were many, especially for the small- and mid-sized departments. It has become important that officer strength reflect the workload and the activity levels in the community. At the same time it is more recognized that officers have family needs and seek more flexibility as in three-day weekends. One accommodation has been ten- or twelve-hour shifts; morale tends to be improved in these settings, and many ten- or twelve-hour day departments indicate their productivity has improved. There is more time off for the officers personal lives, and the department has less downtime for shift changes and between-shifts time losses. Also some agencies change or rotate the working shift infrequently in order to provide officers with more stability in their personal life adjustments.

As unions and collective bargaining units have entered into governmental work, indications are that fringe considerations, working conditions, and specific benefits are now all a part of employee-employer negotiation and contract.

There are other potential costs and expenses that are important to ascertain prior to deciding upon an agency. In some cases all equipment and uniforms are furnished; in others the officer may have to purchase these. Good career planning requires review of these various factors, since many young recruits are not in a position to make heavy initial monetary outlays in order to obtain a job.

Many people believe that one of the greatest advantages of a police career is the regularity and security of employment, particularly in times of economic instability. This security doubtless has attracted applicants over the years and will continue to do so, especially when coupled with the early retirement age and the resulting pension. Many employees, notably those who entered law enforcement careers following World War II and the Korean War, have retired and pursued productive work in second careers. These second careers have ranged from industrial and retail security to college teaching and practicing law. Like military careers, law enforcement offers the advantage of a lifetime pension while one is young enough to engage in further vocational interests; yet as in the military, many individuals remain in law enforcement because promotions have created new opportunities.

In either case the retirement fund is a forced savings account at an attractive interest rate, and it is usually more than matched by the employer. This fund also ensures an income in case of early retirement because of disability, and it provides family benefits in case of premature death. In addition the Public Safety Officers' Death Benefits Program, which began as part of the Crime Control Act of 1968, has been increased. The death benefit paid by the federal government is now $100,000. This legislation also adds a cost-of-living adjustment to the benefit amount. This legislation applies to on-duty, work-related deaths and is for both police and correctional officers. Although retirement and death benefits may not be an officer's greatest concern, it is important to note that law enforcement compares very favorably to other occupations in that regard.

OTHER INCENTIVES

One of the strongest attractions the police service holds for a young, ambitious person is the opportunity to rise through the ranks. Although this opportunity varies considerably, depending on the size of the department and personnel turnover, it is still something that most successful officers seek, because promotion brings higher pay, additional responsibility, and greater prestige. Because most promotions are made from within the organization and almost always occur after the individual has served several years in a particular rank, few outsiders are found in supervisory and command positions. Although enforcement agencies do employ chiefs or commissioners who have not previously served in the organization, the general pattern has been that those at the top have worked their way up through the ranks.

The procedure for advancement generally requires a written examination followed by an oral interview. The federal agencies often include a group interview in order to observe each candidate in a leadership situation. A medical examination often is required prior to promotion.

It is at promotion time when evidence in support of higher education is quite visible. Those officers with solid field experience now have the opportunity to respond to questions that are often gathered from standard textbooks and the current literature. Thus the advantage should be with those who have studied formally; know good operating procedures; demonstrate knowledge of policies, legal cases, and state-of-the-art techniques; and can communicate their responses in a clear and concise manner. Likewise, in an oral interview, a potential commander should be exact and articulate, positive yet reasonable, decisive yet sensitive to others. These traits can be greatly enhanced by the self-confidence and good judgment that higher education encourages. The more advanced promotional exams include demonstration of selected skills.

The development of assessment centers for promotion is considered a promising sign that a greater objectivity and more equitable measuring tool is at hand. Within the assessment process, the promotional candidate is asked to respond to several situations, role-play in a given scenario, and demonstrate what actions would be taken to meet a particular challenge. Trained assessors, predominately command officers, but also civilians, evaluate the candidate's performance in these simulated situations. This process, along with other tests and interviews, becomes a factor in deciding upon promotions. In recent years some excellent selections for police chief and other command level positions involved assessment centers, and more are expected. Business and industry have pioneered the assessment process, along with the federal government, including the FBI. Considering the investment in promoting personnel to top management positions, the expense of defining the tasks to be measured, developing the exercises, and training the assessors would seem quite justified.

The other feature considered in promotion is the system of seniority, which provides points for years of service within the agency. In recent years the seniority system has deceased in favor of the written and oral performances. In the federal agencies, because of the salary scale, it is not as critical that one obtain a promotion in order to receive a pay raise.

In local and state agencies, aside from normal increments, the salary scale is closely aligned to a military rank system, such as corporal, sergeant, lieutenant, captain, and so on. Therefore, promotions are necessary in order to advance to the higher salaries in this field.

In the past few years, opportunities for promotion through lateral entry have been occurring. In other words, a promising senior officer in one department might be offered the job of chief of police in a neighboring community. Moreover, a state police officer or a federal agent could be appointed as a police administrator in an agency other than the one in which prior career experience was obtained.

The important qualities in promotion are not unlike those in any leadership role: sensitivity, leadership, good judgment, dependability, self-confidence, ability to delegate authority, persuasiveness, skill in communicating with and motivating others. One of the most important contributions made by higher education in the law enforcement field has been the intellectual improvement of officers so that they are better equipped to succeed in promotional examinations. One must recognize, too, that most enforcement agencies have requirements relating to the number of years that must be served in a particular rank before one is eligible to compete for the next rank. This is not necessarily a serious restriction; requirements have been reduced gradually as training and education became more acceptable in lieu of lengthy experience. Then too, law enforcement is a young person's occupation, and there is considerable opportunity for upward movement due to early retirements.

Of course, it is virtually impossible to predict a person's chances for reaching a top position—that of a police chief or a sheriff or state police commissioner. Many individuals have achieved these positions with relatively few years in patrol and investigative assignments. Their appointments were based largely upon the leadership and administrative talents they demonstrated in the lower ranks. Top positions, such as sheriff, are generally the direct result of political appointment or election; and many persons would prefer to achieve a command position with direct responsibility for the delivery of services, remaining there for the duration of their career.

In summary we can say with certainty that police salaries exceed those of most other public servants and certain professionals whose credentials have traditionally required higher education. Police officers have higher salaries than do crime lab technicians, probation and parole officers, private sector security officers, detention officers, and case workers. Traditionally, in many local communities, police and firefighter salaries have been linked; partly because the recruitment pool was similar, and partly due to these two positions being supported from the same public safety share of the tax dollar. In situations where the law enforcement salaries are ahead of fire service, it may be due to the higher education incentive monies available to police, or it may come about due to mandated state standards and certification.

In the federal law enforcement agencies, salaries tend to be higher than in local and state government, especially after one attains several years of experience, and guaranteed overtime. Termed administratively "uncontrollable overtime," this payment accrues for federal agents with irregular duty hours.

For the most part, anyone seeking employment in the federal career system will become a part of the government service, General Schedule, pay plan. This system provides for annual pay steps, and employees typically progress one step up the GS scale after each year of service. Pay raises are determined by congressional action and in typical years have averaged between 4 and 5 percent. Agencies vary as to entrance level because of the differences in educational qualifications, specific duties, and types of specialization required. Nonetheless, most federal law enforcement officers will be paid within several of the GS categories described in the following examples. There are jurisdictional differences that exist according to location and cost of living.

Let us consider a GS 7 agent who begins employment with the Drug Enforcement Administration or the Bureau of Alcohol, Tobacco, and Firearms. This typical special agent applicant would possess a bachelor's degree and perhaps some graduate study or investigative experience as well. The new GS 7 can expect to earn $23,171 to start and $26,259 within five years on the same schedule. Many federal agents receive overtime pay, and sometimes that can be as much as 25 percent of their base pay. They can assume that they will travel, work extended daytime duty, be needed on weekends, and all of that will accrue overtime payments.

The GS 9 federal position generally requires the bachelor's degree plus graduate study, a law degree, or as much as five years of related investigative experience. The GS 9 starts at $29,290 under current salary scale, and using our average agent example again, would be earning a base salary of $33,070 after five years. Top step on the GS 9 scale, achieved after ten years of service, would be $37,795 using the current schedule.

In terms of career advancement, we might take the example of a GS 11 who headed a district administrative area and had a dozen years of federal service. An estimated salary for that manager would be $46,000. For a careerist even higher in the administrative structure, perhaps a GS 12, with similar seniority, the salary could reach $55,000. Reviewing this further, it is easy to see how a senior supervisor, with overtime, and normal pay step progressions, could expect to be earning within the range of $50,000 to $60,000. To repeat, pay raises can be expected to be in the 4 percent range as they have been for recent years. Also, federal government employees are now under the Social Security Act in addition to the attractive federal pension system.

Other federal service job benefits are equally attractive, including travel; opportunity for transfer; and one of the better retirement systems available in the employment world, sometimes with provisions for retirement as early as age fifty-five after twenty years service. In fact, retirement at age fifty-five has become more the rule than the exception with federal agents. Other normal fringes include paid vacation and holidays, low cost medical and life insurance, sick leave and financial protection for injury in the line of duty, and special federally supported death benefits. Federal service also affords a measure of employment security that is important to many.

Before concluding the salary discussion on service with the United States government, we should note that for those who reach the top of their agency structure, the earnings rise accordingly. A GS 15, for example, receives a step one base salary of $67,941 and up to $88,300 after ten years service. Deputy administrators, assistant directors, and titles such as those are paid in the range of $90,000. Presidential appointees can earn as much as $129,000.

One variation worth noting is the Federal Bureau of Investigation. That agency begins its special agents at a level GS 10 where the salary is $32,256. Hence, a GS 10 new agent, with administrative uncontrollable overtime (25 percent) would be earning over $40,000. Most FBI agents are in the category of GS 13, which begins at $48,878. Supervisory special agents are started in the GS 14 schedule at over $57,760.

We have now reviewed many of the rewards of a career in law enforcement. Each aspirant must weigh objectives with the many other considerations and think in terms of a career plan. Law enforcement, unlike most other occupations, offers two choices: a steady, long-term commitment with early retirement, or a shorter duration of active duty followed by numerous other endeavors limited only by imagination. Consider the ultimate example: joining a police department or a federal agency at age twenty-one and then retiring after twenty years or even twenty-five years.

The concept of a *career development plan* is receiving widespread attention and some implementation in modern law enforcement organizations. Although not entirely a new idea, the use of such a plan in most criminal justice agencies is rather recent. For many years the military and most federal departments have offered employees a career development approach that embraced special training, varying assignments, and opportunities to be rewarded and recognized according to individual desire and capability.

In years past police career development plans were quite informal and individual, but resulted in many former law enforcement officers leaving their original agency and moving on to become public safety directors, college professors, heads of private security operations, as well as judges, legislators, and mayors. This mobility factor strongly suggests to the young career aspirant that other alternatives will come one's way when an entry job is combined with formal education, relevant training, determination to succeed, and willingness to carefully consider new options. Preparing for retirement and a second career is a truly unique feature of working in criminal justice.

FRUSTRATIONS

Dedicated service to others can be demanding, and police officers are among those who must perform their duties under conditions that are not always comfortable. Nor can such a career be regarded as routine. All jobs, of course, have disadvantages, so in any occupation one can expect to endure some long hours, difficulties in getting ahead, daily frustrations, and disappointments. However, most law enforcement officers must contend with shift rotation, and regardless of experience, it is never psychologically or physiologically easy to start the day's work at midnight. Stress has become a job-related illness that law enforcement administrators and psychologists are trying to prevent and alleviate. Many agencies now offer their employees a training program on nutrition, exercise, and stress-reduction techniques. Few occupations are as demanding on the emotions or as conflicting to one's logic and sense of reason as police work. Behind many of the daily difficulties of police work is *public apathy.* Its causes are numerous and hard to understand, but unfortunately all employees of the criminal justice system feel its impact. The public reflects its apathy through limitations of funds, lack of continuous support, indifference to the causes of crime, refusal to cooperate with authorities, and a frequent disinterest or disenchantment in the police as a unit of government and society.

Public apathy translates itself to the police officer in the form of political leaders who fail to stand behind enforcement actions, a public that demands equal compliance with the law but expects personal immunity, and the lost personal idealism of those officers sworn to uphold all laws, only to discover that citizens really expect something less of them.

Social alienation and citizen distrust continue to be major officer frustrations and can cause attitudinal changes as officers encounter them too frequently. The continuing efforts to maintain community policing and citizen involvement are strategies designed to counteract this "we/they" syndrome. There are acceptable mechanisms for coping with job and organizational stress, and the wise leadership in any organization makes every effort to reduce the consequences of known stressors.

THE ELEMENT OF DANGER

An element of danger always exists in the life of a peace officer, and there is ample evidence that physical attacks on officers have increased in recent years. Dedicated guardians of the peace feel the physical risks are outweighed by the advantages of challenge, excitement, and working under a vast array of circumstances, often outdoors. However, any confrontation with people under stress, whether in a family quarrel or at a holdup scene, is a potentially dangerous one that calls for physical and emotional courage. And there are no substitutes for good judgment, intensive training, and wearing body armor.

Anyone considering a career in law enforcement must recognize that, as the visible symbol of authority in the community, he or she may become the target of those choosing to react against established order. The risk is ever-present, but statistics suggest that considering the many thousands of daily encounters between police and the public, relatively few end in injury or loss of life. Training and determined professional bearing equip the officer to deal with hazardous situations. The fact that many police injuries and deaths occur through traffic accidents, stopping vehicles whose occupants are unknown, and domestic arguments is strong evidence that thorough training and disciplined caution are essential.

The number of law enforcement officers killed in the line of duty tends to remain in a fairly constant state. Looking back to 1986, feloniously slain officers numbered 66, the lowest number since the late 1960s. The figure for 1987 was 74; the number for 1988 was 78. In 1992 that figure dropped to 63 but climbed again in 1993 to 70 officers.

Another point of significance is that drug-related arrests now account for increasing police deaths, but the majority are still due to arrest situations and investigating suspicious persons or circumstances.

Unfortunately an equal number of officers lose their lives due to accidents, with fifty-nine killed in vehicular crashes, including motorcycles and aircraft, and struck by vehicles in 1993. In 1992 the accidental deaths numbered 66.

Assaults on officers continue to be a severe problem, and police officers must use extreme caution in dealing with an unknown situation. But one must keep these losses in context and recognize that twenty-four hours of every day, police officers are in contact with every imaginable circumstance in their community.

A police officer must constantly deal with human suffering, but, unlike most citizens, the officer cannot permit personal emotions to take control. The job demands that one always maintain self-control, act with calm efficiency, and display confidence and courage—while never appearing to lack compassion. Officers face difficulty and tragedy daily, and no matter how hard they may try, the police are often unable to prevent them. This dilemma constitutes the emotional burden of a police officer's work, where personal safety is always at stake.

Visible public support for the police varies according to the real level of concern that citizens have for the particular laws being enforced. There exists full public cooperation and support for police actions surrounding the kidnapping of a child; less but increasing amounts for drunken driving arrests; and minimal support for strict enforcement of the laws prohibiting gambling.

Criminal Justice System Costs, 1990

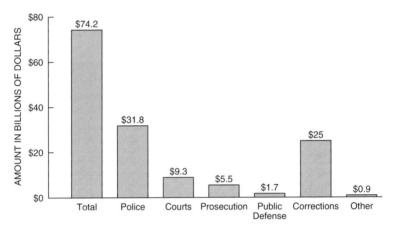

Source: U.S. Department of Justice, Bureau of Justice Statistics, *Justice Expenditure and Employment, 1990,* (Washington, DC: U.S. Government Printing Office, September 1992).

CHAPTER 6

EDUCATIONAL REQUIREMENTS

In years past there has been a determined effort by local governmental officials to demand that all police applicants be high school graduates. According to the President's Crime Commission (1967), more than 70 percent of the nation's police departments required a high school diploma for employment. Beyond that, police departments in nine states and more than thirty departments in California alone raised their standards to require some successful completion of college work. The state of California, effective in 1970, announced that six college credits would be required of all its future peace officers. Other enforcement agencies in such diverse locations as Flint, Michigan; Wichita, Kansas; Arlington, Virginia; Madison, Wisconsin; Bellevue, Washington; Dallas, Texas; and the Washington and Texas Highway Patrols have been giving priority to the completion of two years of college for entrance. By the mid-1980s over 90 percent of all local police agencies were requiring the high school diploma, and in many settings college credits are awarded as part of the recruit basic training program. Several states, notably Michigan and Minnesota, have developed college level studies as part of their certified training system and, hence, all new recruits gain educational experience as part of their state certification process. That has been true in California for many years, and is also increasingly true in Florida and Texas. Moreover there are further indications that a number of major police agencies will move beyond the associate degree requirement, particularly for specialized, technical, and command positions.

The future will certainly call for some satisfactory college study prior to entrance into police service. Part of the reason for this trend is the fact that more and more young people will be attending colleges, particularly local community colleges, in the coming decades. Even if law enforcement did not actively recruit for such sources, there would be a gradual tendency to attract new personnel with exposure to higher education. Moreover, in 1973, the National Advisory Commission on Criminal Justice Standards and Goals recommended that, by 1982, every police agency should require a four-year college degree as a condition of initial employment. This projection was given considerable impetus by the fact that over 500 community and junior colleges offer associate degree programs in this career field, and beyond the associate level, there are many universities that offer a bachelor's degree in police administration, corrections, or criminal justice. The projections and national recommendations were made at a time when employment and economic conditions looked favorable; with inflation and hiring limits, the academic requirements have been slowed, but there is much evidence that higher education has become commonplace within police departments, and most major communities can expect to have a number of recruits with college backgrounds from now on.

Graduate degrees in criminal justice are increasingly available and may be obtained in law enforcement or in the related academic fields of public administration, criminology, or corrections. The growing availability of two-year, four-year, and graduate programs in law enforcement suggests the importance of considering college preparation prior to entering criminal justice at the local, state, or federal level.

Costs for the various programs in institutions of higher learning vary significantly. Generally speaking, the local community college is less expensive for area students; the state colleges and universities cost somewhat more. The out-of-state student will, of course, pay more to attend any of these institutions. It is wise to obtain a school catalog, and, if distance permits, to get an appointment with the director of the college criminal justice program. If no specific law enforcement or corrections degree program is available, the prospective student should contact the general counselors in the institution about an appropriate course of study.

For persons who do not have access to a specialized degree program, related areas of study might include public administration, sociology, political science, psychology, computer science, and business management.

Agencies that have acknowledged the need for higher education among police officers frequently use college educational attainment as a criterion for hiring. Kansas City, Missouri, reports that they only hire personnel with about two years of college credits and have therefore been able to increase the academic requirements for promotion. Police agencies in Montgomery County, Maryland; Arlington County, Virginia; and Tallahassee, Coral Gables, and Gainesville, Florida, all require that applicants possess two years of higher education. Because of the manner in which new recruits receive their police training, Minnesota has set a job requisite of two years of college.

Departments have established a college education as a requirement to take promotional exams, as in Ann Arbor, Michigan, and Des Moines, Iowa; or as a part of the police cadet experience prior to being employed as an officer; or as a part of the recruit training program, as in Dade County, Florida, where that training is an integral part of the community college. This arrangement has been true in Chicago for many years where recruits obtain college credits as a part of their training experience. Chicago now requires two years of college credit before hiring.

Nearly all police agencies require a high school diploma for entrance, and between 16 to 18 percent of police departments have some higher education requirement for employment. Only .5 percent of agencies require more than two years. The serious student interested in a law enforcement career should seek out organizations with policies that support the pursuit of higher education. One should inquire about financial support for job-related tuition costs, or an informal policy of promoting those who have college credit.

In a 1990 survey by the Police Executive Research Forum, the average educational level of police officers was found to be two years of college, and there is every indication that this trend began well over a decade ago and is continuing. Given the circumstances in the late 1960s, (average officer at the twelfth-grade level), the large number of officers involved, and the amount of time required for social change, the progress is impressive.

Whether they enroll in a local community college, attend a university, or enter policing while still in school, the message is clear: It is wise for students to begin their education as early as possible rather than waiting until their careers have been underway for years. Many have done so, but delaying educational development makes it more difficult for officers to achieve their goals.

HIGH SCHOOL

Some subjects in the high school curriculum will prove especially useful for a career in public service or law enforcement. They include American government, civics, sociology, psychology, and any other courses that deal with the social and human institutions. Such a student might also be encouraged to pursue mathematics to develop deductive reasoning powers. Laboratory sciences that teach the importance of observing, recording, and accurate reporting are also helpful. The communications arts, learned through the study of writing, literature, and public speaking, are very important. In high schools where business law or other legal subjects are available, the law enforcement career aspirant would be well advised to study this crucial information. In addition, some police officers find skill in typing to be most useful. With the addition of computers into most agencies, a working knowledge of that field has also become advantageous. Some high schools now offer a course in criminal justice or law enforcement, and anyone interested in such a career should take these courses.

COLLEGE

A student nearing completion of high school should obtain catalogs from several community colleges or universities offering a criminal justice degree in order to become familiar with specific entrance requirements. Some of these institutions will require that potential law enforcement majors demonstrate qualifications beyond simply possessing a high school diploma. It is not generally regarded as desirable for colleges to establish rigid physical requirements for entrance into these specialized programs. However, students should recognize the requirements of physical, character, and background investigations conducted by police agencies before an applicant is employed. Students should remember that a college degree in law enforcement does not necessarily guarantee employment as a sworn police officer in the agency of one's choice. For this reason, requirements for admission to college programs vary throughout the country.

Described below is a suggested balanced curriculum for both law enforcement and corrections associate degree students. These curricula represent revisions of those prepared by the author several years ago under a Kellogg Foundation Grant to the American Association of Community and Junior Colleges. They have been altered slightly to accommodate recent trends within community colleges and the criminal justice career field.

LAW ENFORCEMENT CURRICULUM SUMMARY
(Associate Degree)

First Year

General Education Courses:
  English/Technical Report Writing
  Psychology
  Sociology/Criminology
  Government

Technical, Specialized Courses:
  Introduction to Law Enforcement/
    Criminal Justice
  Police Organization/Administra-
    tion/Operations/Procedures
  Juvenile Delinquency Prevention/
    Procedures/Control
  Criminal Law

Second Year

General Education Courses:
  Math
  Humanities/Social Science

Technical, Specialized Courses:
  Police Supervision
  Criminal Investigation
  Law of Evidence (Procedure)
  Police Community Relations/Hu-
    man Relations
  Introduction to Criminalistics
  Internship/Practicum/Field
    Experience
  Seminar: Topics

Most typical additional specialized courses include:
Traffic Administration/Control/Regulation
Administration of Justice (Emphasis on Courts and Legal Process)
Narcotics/Drug Abuse/Investigation
Computers and Their Usage
Cultural and Ethnic Diversity

The associate degree program in corrections is presented for those persons interested in working with offenders and being a part of the treatment and rehabilitation process. (For details see Chapter 7.)

CORRECTIONS CURRICULUM SUMMARY
(Associate Degree)
First Year

General Education Courses:
  English/Technical Report Writing
  Psychology
  Sociology/Penology
  Government

Second Year

General Education Courses:
  Math
  Humanities/Social Science
  Abnormal Psychology/Collective
    or Deviant Behavior

Technical, Specialized Courses:
 Introduction to Corrections
 Correctional Institutions
 Juvenile Delinquency/Procedures
 Criminal Law/Correctional Law

Technical, Specialized Courses:
 Correctional Administration
 Interviewing/Counseling
 Community-based Corrections/
  Treatment/Rehabilitation
 Probation and Parole
 Internship/Practicum/Field
  Experience
 Crisis Intervention
 Correctional Supervision

Most typical additional specialized courses include:
 Cultural and Ethnic Diversity
 Administration of Justice (Emphasis on Courts and Legal Process)
 Substance Abuse

Communications skills should be mastered at the community college level for those preparing for university level study. Likewise, a community college student should take advantage of courses in the social and behavioral sciences in order to better understand the problems, stresses, and dilemmas encountered by the justice system and its representatives.

Bachelor's Degree in Administration of Justice/Criminal Justice

To plan for study at the university level, one should first obtain cata- logs from institutions offering specialized programs with the appropriate balance of academic preparation in related fields of study. Persons with higher education find that opportunities arise as their careers progress, and it is always wise to obtain some knowledge base beyond the specialized major. Thus, the law enforcement (criminal justice) major may look to business management and computer science for electives or even a minor field of study; the corrections major would do well to develop counseling and other social work skills; the juvenile justice major might study rehabilitation or education to augment a resourceful career.

Many faculty members feel strongly that a criminal justice major, broadly based, is excellent preparation for law school, social work, or public administration. If the career goal is criminalistics, that is, the science of laboratory examinations or research, then an entirely different undergraduate preparation is called for—one in chemistry, biology, or physics with strong preparation in mathematics and computers. An undergraduate major in the administration of justice should assist the university student in developing knowledge and skills needed by an effective practitioner.

Before selecting a bachelor's program, one should determine that it is going to provide a well-rounded knowledge of the discipline and the specialty desired. This means that the curriculum must address underlying concepts, theories, and principles but also present the state of the art in terms of practice. The program must also prepare the student to address problems and complex issues, to employ proper research skills, and to evaluate, analyze, and synthesize issues that confront the field.

Assuming that the university student transfers from a community college where some specialization has been available, and that the fundamentals have already been received, then listed below are suggestions for an upper division academic experience. Of course, if the university student enters the senior institution as a freshman, the curriculum would still involve introductory courses, criminal law, investigation, and some of the others mentioned previously. (Areas of study listed below describe the subject and are not necessarily course titles.)

LAW ENFORCEMENT (POLICE) OPTION OR SPECIALIZATION

Administration, Planning & Management
Economic Offenses/Organized Crime
Industrial & Retail (Private) Security
Theories and Practices in Police Agencies
Strategies for Crime & Delinquency Prevention
Case Studies in Legal Evidence & Procedures
Criminalistics & Crime Analysis
Human Behavior in Criminal Justice

CORRECTIONS (TREATMENT AND REHABILITATION)

Administration (Adult & Juvenile)
Community-Based Corrections Programming
Correctional Law
Evaluation & Treatment of Offenders
Counseling & Therapeutic Techniques

JUVENILE JUSTICE

Juvenile Justice Law & Process
Strategies for Crime & Delinquency Prevention
Courses related to Behavior, Treatment, & Administration cited above

In addition to the specialization courses, there are common core ones that reflect information necessary for anyone entering the justice system with a bachelor's degree. These might be described as follows:

Courts and Judicial Process
Crime and Delinquency Prevention
Planning and Resource Analysis
Criminal Justice Research
Comparative Justice Systems
Critical Issues or Topic Seminars
Field Experience/Internships
Criminological Theories

Additional upper division skills, not necessarily obtained solely through criminal justice departments, but clearly relevant to career planning, are:

Research & Evaluation Techniques
Policy Analysis and Public Administration
Information Systems/Computer Sciences
Accounting and Auditing Procedures
Counseling & Treatment Techniques

Criminal justice majors should consider a minor in such departments as sociology, psychology, urban planning, public administration, social work, political science, computer sciences, or business management and information systems. For the laboratory major, the minors would be physical sciences or mathematics. Emerging specializations that are justice related can be found in more and more colleges and universities. These might include fire safety and fire science, private security and loss prevention, and traffic and transportation safety; there are also degrees entirely devoted to occupational, home, and recreational safety. There are new courses in topics such as industrial, retail, and business security and computer security and risk management. Only a few years ago, few would have anticipated academic course titles such as environmental protection and enforcement; human factors and environmental stresses; loss control management; planning for change in criminal justice; alternatives to incarceration; drugs, alcohol and crime; and victimology. An excellent combination of such programs can be found in some state universities, and a student might consider a major combining the justice and safety fields. Those considering law school might mix justice and safety topics with government and business studies. Before making a final decision, a serious student should obtain catalogs from well-established and well-recognized universities in this field. Seek out their course descriptions and options for combining areas and then proceed according to what these programs provide in breadth. Depending upon the location of the country that appeals to you, broadly based curricula can be found at the following institutions of higher learning:

Eastern Kentucky University
Southern Illinois University
Michigan State University
Sam Houston State University
Virginia Commonwealth University
Indiana University
Florida State University
American University
California State University–Fresno
University of Illinois at Chicago
University of South Carolina
Georgia State University
Arizona State University
Indiana University of Pennsylvania
California State University–Sacramento
California State University–Long Beach
Central Missouri State University
University of Maryland
Northeastern University
University of Nebraska–Omaha
John Jay College of Criminal Justice–New York City
University of Louisville
Washington State University
Appalachian State University
Rutgers University
Auburn University
Wichita State University

Many more than those named above offer criminal justice degrees, but by reviewing catalogs and program options from some with comprehensive programs, a student can begin to see the potential for a career. One might want to combine public and private sector courses; another might wish to combine legal and investigative courses with fire safety and fire protection; still another student could mix traffic safety with research and analysis; while another may want a more traditional law enforcement emphasis but with additional studies in laboratory procedures and crime scene analysis. Review the catalogs and then discuss the possibilities with faculty advisors, family members, and especially with persons currently employed in various aspects and levels of the justice and safety systems.

In every state now there are also graduate degree programs; one can obtain a master's degree (30–36 credits) with concentration in policy, management, administration, research, or correctional treatment. Persons with graduate training typically enter teaching, research, mid-level management, and some of the newer occupations involving planning, project direction, and organizational analysis. Doctorates are also available in public administration, criminology, and criminal justice, all of which generally lead to teaching and research.

CADET PROGRAM—A WORK-STUDY PLAN

The cooperative training aspects of many occupational education programs have, for the most part, not yet been included in law enforcement programs. Instead, on-the-job training has been provided for preservice students through informal arrangements worked out between the police student and the law enforcement agency. The absence of large numbers of formal work-study arrangements probably results from hesitancy on the part of the community college to involve students in what is perceived as a potentially hazardous experience.

In any event, most law enforcement educational programs do not yet provide work experience as a part of the formal educational process. However, some students gain law enforcement experience during their college careers through full or part-time employment with a local agency as a records clerk, typist, or other civilian employee. Such work experience is rarely assessed and bears little resemblance to the carefully supervised and evaluated internship period associated with other occupational programs.

It is essential that greatly expanded law enforcement work experience programs be established in the future. The community college can make a significant contribution to such programs because of its proximity to occupational life in the community. Community colleges can help the student get on-the-job experience that makes classroom work realistic and increases motivation. In addition to these advantages to the individual, work programs ensure that the college curricula is being tested each day in the actual work environment. Through the combined efforts of such organizations as the International Association of Chiefs of Police and the American Association of Community and Junior Colleges, a dramatic increase in work experience programs in law enforcement is forecast in the years ahead.*

The concept of the *police cadet* is by no means new, and the program now appears to be gaining momentum throughout the nation. The basic purpose of police cadet programs is to facilitate police recruitment by employing youths aged seventeen to twenty who demonstrate superior potential for police careers, but who are below the minimum age requirement.

In some communities they have been given such titles as community service officer or public safety aides, but the concept is to help young people enter related careers early and gain experience while attending college. The medical field and various high technology areas of industry do this regularly, and the process provides for a steady flow of motivated and educated persons into an occupational specialty.

Many large cities, including New York City, Chicago, Miami, Washington, DC, Detroit, Baltimore, New Orleans, and St. Louis have established such programs and generally report considerable satisfaction with them. The cadet program is not limited to the large city. Smaller communities also have manpower requirements that can be met by persons not possessing sworn police powers. For further information young career aspirants should contact department administrators within their region to learn whether such an opportunity exists.

In all locations cadets work, they attend classes, they play on their own teams in the police department league, and they look forward to the

---

Guidelines for Work Experience Programs in the Criminal Justice System, by Jimmy C. Styles and Denny F. Pace. American Association of Community and Junior Colleges, 1 Dupont Circle, NW, Washington, DC 20036.

day they can qualify for appointments as patrol officers. They have the potential, individually and as a group, to make important contributions to the department. The program keeps them involved in police procedures through the critical years between graduation from high school and their twenty-first birthdays.

In every locale cadets work in accordance with departmental policies and procedures and the provisions of a departmental training program. They are subject to specific assignment and instruction as well as frequent review of work by supervisors. Trainees participate in a departmental program of instruction in modern police methods and duties and perform a variety of miscellaneous prepatrol duties. They also are responsible for performing routine clerical duties such as typing, filing, and preparing police forms and records; operating a telephone switchboard and recording hourly calls from and relaying instructions to street patrol officers; maintaining records of all arrests and missing persons; recording change of address for vehicle operators' licenses.

In some cities cadets or aides may work a full forty-hour week at their departmental jobs. Their work is a form of training; they are learning departmental procedures and are becoming acquainted with key departmental functions. Cadets are rotated among various assignments at six-month intervals in order to become familiar with many aspects of departmental operations.

In addition cadets are required to carry six units per semester in police studies or related subjects. This training is to be accomplished on their own time before or after regular working hours.

Cadets are required to furnish and wear a uniform that is very similar to that worn by the regular departmental officers. The cost of the uniform is borne by the cadet.

At age twenty-one, cadets are eligible to take an examination for advancement to police patrol status. A "promotional" eligible list takes priority over the "open" eligible list regularly used in filling police patrol positions. Thus, all successful cadets should be able to become police patrol officers as soon as they reach the necessary age.

RECRUIT TRAINING

All newly appointed law enforcement officers receive some form of initial training prior to being assigned to their duties. In general, recruits in the federal, state, and metropolitan jurisdictions are assigned to an organized training program that may last from eight to ten weeks up to six months. New officers in smaller communities may not have equal opportunity to prepare for service, although most are permitted to enroll in academies operated by the large cities or the state agency. Fortunately, new statewide training courses are being made available to more officers than ever before—in some places through the junior and community college systems, and in other places through regionally distributed academy facilities.

As state minimum standards legislation now exists everywhere, local and state officers must attain whatever certification is required. Thus, whether the training be offered by local departments, in a regional academy, or in a centralized state setting, all states have some form of minimum requirements and curriculum that must be successfully completed. The content and minimum number of hours of required recruit (basic) training varies around the nation. Some states mandate as few as 260 or 280 class hours, but these are rapidly becoming fewer and fewer. The 1990s emerged with a minimum basic requirement in some states more like 400 hours as a norm. There are states with minimum requirements over 500 hours; these include California, Florida, Pennsylvania, and Connecticut. Keep in mind that these figures are required minimum hours of training and many jurisdictions will exceed their state minimums. The increasing hours in the last 25 years bring with them the message that professional status for sworn law enforcement officers has arrived in most states. Recognizing that in the 1960s few states provided any legislation for police training, the 1970s brought state legislation as low as 120–160 hours, and the average was about 200 hours until nearly 1980, the growth and accomplishment in this arena is remarkable.

Beyond requirements for recruit training, new emphasis is being placed upon supervisory development so that those promoted to sergeant will have a thorough knowledge of their jobs. In the middle management ranks, such as lieutenant, it is vital that new instruction be offered because patrol and investigative experiences cannot prepare one sufficiently for command assignments. And officials in the top command positions, regardless of street experience, require training in budgeting, planning, and organizational efficiency. No easy method exists for delivering this necessary knowledge to the various assignments, and so we find that a variety of training courses is available, but not necessarily equally throughout the nation.

Recruit training curricula vary among the local and state agencies, particularly with regard to local ordinances, rules, and regulations; use of departmental equipment; and report forms. However, all such training includes lectures and demonstrations on first responder (emergency medical aid), criminal and traffic investigations, traffic control, patrol procedures, legal terms and criminal laws, courtroom testimony, procedures in handling disputes, search and seizure rules, writing citations, and many other subject areas related to police duties. The recruit can also expect to spend considerable time on the firing range, learning the service weapon, shotgun, and other weapons in the agency arsenal, including chemical agents. Likewise, the gymnasium will be used for the fitness program and for learning defensive tactics and search and restraint techniques. Operation of the police vehicle will be taught on the driving range, and this usually includes learning to control the vehicle in difficult situations. The more time that can be dedicated to practical exercises, simulations, and being tested by proving one's competencies, the better will be the final graduate of the training academy.

CAREER DEVELOPMENT AND IN-SERVICE TRAINING

The modern police training environment will include presentations about diverse cultural groups, techniques for resolving disputes, officer survival and safety considerations, victim and witness assistance, discretionary and judgmental weapons usage, conducting field sobriety tests, and computer usage.

There is a great deal to be taught in limited class time so schedules are strict, complete note taking generally is required, and a disciplined atmosphere may prevail. Some departments are rescheduling their recruit training to give new officers an opportunity for field experience in conjunction with classroom study.* In recent years, the number of nonpolice personnel employed by police academies has increased, although

---

Law Enforcement Training and the Community College, by Denny F. Pace, James D. Stinchcomb, and Jimmie C. Styles. American Association of Community and Junior Colleges, 1 Dupont Circle, NW, Washington, DC 20036.

most lecturers are law enforcement personnel. Experienced agency personnel bring considerable background to the course they instruct, while holding operating costs to a minimum. Guest lecturers are, however, essential. They come from federal agencies, the courts, and a variety of local agencies with which the police regularly deal.

Examples of guest lecturers who could be considered critical to police training are attorneys from the prosecution office; arson investigators from the fire department; investigators from the medical examiner's office; and commanders of special units such as helicopter, canine, tactical or swat.

Local community colleges and universities frequently assist police academies by offering instruction on criminology, delinquency, psychology, report writing, human behavior, communications, supervision, computer usage, and other academic topics relating to police work. The future will continue to see more academic preparation being incorporated into police training and an increase in the opportunity to obtain college credits for studies in the recruit training program.

Most police training includes some exposure to audiovisual techniques and training films because new officers must have the opportunity to observe as much as possible before facing real-life situations. To that end, they will also be required to demonstrate automobile driving habits, participate in a simulated crime scene search, testify in a mock trial, and practice such skills as lifting fingerprints and taking photographs. The grading system varies among departments, but tests occur regularly, and students who do not show promise of success can expect to be dropped from the academy. Their grades and efficiency ratings become a part of their permanent personnel record.

State and federal training programs for recruits are often longer than those for local agencies. They also usually reflect better facilities and a larger budget for this important purpose. Of course, training is designed to accommodate the needs of the particular organization, so that highway patrol officers will focus greater attention on the motor vehicle code and accident investigation, while federal agents will concentrate on the statutes that will be their ultimate responsibility. All, however, have some aspects in common, such as defensive tactics, firearms usage, prisoner searches, handling of physical evidence, courtroom demeanor, and preparing accurate reports.

Depending upon the type of agency, recruits also spend many hours studying criminal and constitutional laws, community relations and citizen respect, handling of disturbances, proper radio procedures, basic investigations, and how to recognize and respond to various emergencies. Today's police recruits are also being informed as to their own needs in terms of mental health and stress reduction and the importance of relaxation, positive outlook, good nutrition, and exercise.

The modern police academy, whatever its duration and setting, emphasizes performance and the ability to demonstrate that tasks are understood and can be accomplished. Competency-based or performance-based training, as they are often termed by military schools, are the methods most likely to prove that a recruit can actually save a life through CPR or other procedure, and not simply answer a question about it on an exam. Demonstrating the technique for stopping a vehicle, searching a building, or removing an assailant's weapon means more than writing about it. Through videotaping the exercises and using simulated situations, the new officer obtains a realism previously unknown in the academy.

Again, dependent upon the size of the jurisdiction, the minimum state requirements, and the agency's philosophy, a police trainee might be required to complete as many as 800 to 1,000 hours of basic subjects. It is common to find situations where the state standards dictate only 400 hours and the regional academy or the agency training bureau makes two or three times that number available to newly employed recruits.

Minnesota has set progressive standards and has become, along with California and Florida, a pacesetter in certification requirements. Since 1977 Minnesota officers must take at least two years of training, either through a vocational-technical program or in a college. Both academic subjects and required skills are covered. Every three years, to maintain certification, the officer in Minnesota must complete another forty-eight hours of state-approved training.

Michigan is another progressive state where higher education is linked with recruit training for police, and requirements are above the national norm.

In Texas, at Sam Houston State, as in Florida, at several regional training centers including Miami, special programs combine academic requirements with the complete recruit certification academy. Hence one completing these types of programs is eligible for employment throughout the state.

In Minnesota applicants and officers-to-be may choose to enter a certified two-year program during which they must also complete the job-related skills course and the state licensing examination. The other alternative is a certified vocational-technical school that includes both academic and job-related skills. Again, after the licensing exam, the applicant must locate employment within the state. Under both of these methods, the individual, rather than the hiring agency, bears the cost of the education and training. Other states and regions have been reviewing similar approaches since they are so cost effective.

The advent of the written state examination is yet another effort at attaining professional stature for law enforcement. A number of states, including Illinois, California, Texas, Michigan, Minnesota, and Florida all now require successful completion of a state mandated competence examination prior to sworn status employment.

In Florida, the certified officer must complete an additional forty hours of approved training within each four-year span. Other states also have various training requirements for those already employed and in service.

Some of the topics in recruit training have been mentioned previously, but let us look at what else one must learn prior to entering police service:

- The role of environmental protection agencies and how pollution control is enforced.
- Expectation of law enforcement in terms of ethics and standards of conduct. Legal terminology should be mastered, as well as statutes and basic laws of arrest.
- Public speaking, report writing, and nonverbal communications are all crucial.
- Sensitivity to various groups, be they minority, handicapped, elderly, or young and the many facets of drug abuse, alcoholism, and mental illness that one encounters.
- Firefighting as well as recognizing hazards and risks during routine patrol.
- Dealing with traffic problems, including drunken drivers, congestion, or crashes.
- Interviewing and routine preliminary investigative techniques and procedures.

- Crisis intervention skills and proper approaches to calls for service.
- Proper use of the firearm, baton, handcuffs, and unarmed defense techniques.
- Managing conflicts and disturbances that arise in neighborhoods and families. Domestic violence.
- Understanding and dealing with tensions and issues that require resolution. Community and problem-solving police strategies.
- Maintaining an alert and safety-conscious status at all times.

Following completion of their formal classroom studies, most enforcement officers are assigned to work under the supervision of an experienced officer who must evaluate the new employee's performance periodically. In addition to a supervisor, the recruit may work with a more experienced partner for a time to receive instruction in specific methods and procedures and to ensure that all efforts are in line with departmental policy. Of course, the effectiveness of such procedures depends upon the personnel involved, but all departments agree on the importance of on-the-job training for recruits.

The probation period generally begins upon entrance into the recruit training program. It may continue for at least one year; in some agencies it lasts for two years. During that period, the new officer receives not only classroom instruction, but also field training and supervised on-the-job experience. This transition period is critical to detecting deficiencies in the selection process as well as limitations in the classroom training program.

After the police recruit has worked under the guidance of the field training officers, as they are often termed, he or she is eligible for full status as a patrol officer. Performance evaluation continues as officers must now rely on their own judgment rather than the classroom or an experienced supervisor. Most police administrators feel strongly that observing their performance is the best way to evaluate whether new recruits are suited for a police career. Such views are strongly supported by the fact that the stresses and conflicts of enforcement work cannot adequately be simulated, and, therefore, one must perform duties before being assigned permanent status as a police officer.

In some agencies the probation period is spent rotating from one major division to another to become acquainted with the entire organization. Ideally, performance ratings during the probation period will be frequent, classroom retraining will occur, and conferences with supervisors will be scheduled on a regular basis. In addition, training evaluation from the recruits is becoming increasingly important to the training academy in order to ensure basic training meets on-the-job needs.

Formal licensing and certification for law enforcement officers occurs when they are sworn in to their positions, take the oath of office, and are awarded a badge. As mentioned previously, the state also then certifies them as adequately trained and authorized to serve. In all jurisdictions the badge is the symbol of legal authority, and with it comes the power of detaining, arrest, and other responsibilities for community safety and security. The uniform and badge also symbolize that one is the visible representative of government and authority, and in a democracy this is an important point to recognize when considering the implications of a career choice.

As state licensing standards increase, and higher education becomes even more a part of police career development, the profession can be proud of the early developments in California, under their Peace Officer Standards and Training Commission, which undertook the task of setting standards in the mid-1960s. At the same time both New York and New Jersey were enacting legislation of the same type, so law enforcement has had state legislation regarding certification and training standards for more than thirty years in some locales. In Florida, more than in any other state, there is also a legal decertification process for those who do not meet the expectations of agency regulation and state statute.

More officers are also being offered in-service training at an advanced level to ensure up-to-date knowledge and skills. Again, as with recruit training, states are beginning to mandate advanced courses for those who expect to be specialists or to be promoted. Most agencies have encouraged career development study in the past, even when conducted briefly and within the department itself.

The subjects may range from handling the mentally disturbed to recent court decisions, but the purpose is to keep officers current, alert, and informed. One of the most effective methods for giving in-service training to all officers is often termed "roll-call training." This technique, a fifteen-minute daily coverage of the practical aspects of policing, was offered in the Los Angeles Police Department in 1948. The information has been published in book form, and today these manuals are used in other police departments throughout the country.

In 1964, the International Association of Chiefs of Police began publishing a twice-monthly *Training Key.* Available to all members of an agency at low cost, it covers a variety of practical police subjects. Each issue deals with a specific topic, such as searching a suspect, handling the mentally ill, or stopping a vehicle. The *Training Key* has proven quite successful across the nation, since few departments could afford the research and production costs necessary to produce similar publications of their own.

There also are many opportunities to participate in specialized training through institutes and short courses. These may be provided by community colleges, universities, federal agencies, or by the local departments themselves. Officers assigned to certain specialties must receive training that equips them to deal more effectively with their particular area of concern. Any specialized operation demands greater competence, and police officers cannot assume that experience alone can provide that knowledge.

Courses that occur most frequently include those aimed at specialists in juvenile, violent crimes, criminal investigation, traffic, and more recently, computer use, narcotics, community relations, and planning. In addition, there are programs for those who have the training responsibilities for their departments. A training calendar is provided monthly through the IACP's *Police Chief Magazine.* However, there are several agencies and institutions of higher learning that offer regular, well-established programs varying in length from several weeks to several months.

The National Academy, conducted by the Federal Bureau of Investigation, is perhaps the most noteworthy program conducted by a federal agency. This twelve-week session has been operating since the 1930s, and officers from throughout the fifty states as well as many foreign countries are selected to attend. The National Academy has had a significant percentage of its graduates become top level administrators in enforcement agencies over the years.

The Northwestern University Traffic Institute (1804 Hinman Avenue, Evanston, Illinois) affords a variety of specialized courses for enforcement personnel. The nine-month course is particularly concerned with traffic management and police administration. In addition to the long course, there are a number of two- and three-week sessions devoted to various topics such as supervision, accident investigation, and traffic techniques.

The University of North Florida, in Jacksonville, operates The Institute of Police Technology and Management and offers unique courses in resource management, budget planning, use of minicomputers, and other topics that are related to traffic, radar, procedures, and record analysis.

The University of Louisville (Louisville, Kentucky) has operated the Southern Police Institute for more than three decades. Originally developed to assist officers throughout the Southeast, it now accepts applicants from agencies throughout the nation. It also provides a variety of two-week programs with a special three-month course for in-service, supervisory, and command personnel.

The National Crime Prevention Institute, created in 1971, also operates from the School of Justice Administration at the University of Louisville and offers various courses for persons concerned with crime prevention and security.

Several federal agencies conduct specialized courses for local and state law enforcement officers. These include courses on narcotics investigations, hostage and terrorist tactics, explosives and bombs, and surveillances. Currently, many of these are available at the Federal Law Enforcement Training Center in Glynco, Georgia. This is where most federal agents receive training, and it also offers specialty programs to other jurisdictions. The Glynco center does particularly unique work in high risk topics such as officer survival, executive protection, driver training and crash avoidance, hazardous materials, and computer security.

Throughout this chapter we have considered the great importance of career preparation. Considering one's high school electives, selecting an agency with up-to-date training, and seeking out additional in-service study and higher education is most important. The law enforcement community affords personnel numerous opportunities for one-day or one-week training, and the wise employee looks ahead to these and seeks them out. Criminal Justice is too broad a field of endeavor, and includes too many new directions, for anyone to consider stopping after high school. The local community college or state university must be the next step in order to prepare properly for working with our social order. Law enforcement training gives one the organizational setting and the formal authority to take charge of situations and to make decisions that really count.

CHAPTER 7

RELATED CAREERS IN CRIMINAL JUSTICE AND PUBLIC SAFETY

A number of career opportunities are available throughout the administration of justice and public safety systems. Although law enforcement is the most visible and the phase that most citizens recognize, it is by no means the only vocation concerned with the problems of crime and delinquency. Because the police are instantly identified, and their actions are the most reported and commented about, it is no wonder that people thinking about careers focus upon that sector. The fact remains that many other jobs exist throughout public safety, and this chapter will attempt to describe and assess them as logical alternatives.

Career goals require some early planning, and such factors as higher education, physical characteristics, personal determination, and often family and teacher advice will play a part in setting those directions. Some of the readers of this book, while thinking about law enforcement generally, will want to seek out further information about related endeavors. The student who is interested and successful in high school chemistry and physics should look at the world of criminalistics as it relates to an interest in crime solving. Likewise, the student interested in political science, logic, and government may prefer a career in criminal law. It is important to think of the justice and safety systems as an interlocking group of enterprises with common goals. The paths one chooses to help our society to attain those goals may differ, just as many vocational choices exist within the wide field of medical services. There are important choices to be made, and gathering accurate information is the first step.

This section will discuss law as a profession, with the specializations that affect the justice system directly: criminalistics and the forensic crime laboratory, the broad field of corrections and rehabilitation, and the increasing, fast-changing business of private security, loss reduction, and specialized protection services.

The practice of law is perhaps the most obvious pursuit of a related career field. This book will have little to say about the legal profession, since there is a publication on opportunities in law careers that should be obtained by anyone who is thinking about law as a career.* A number of legal officers are participants in the justice system, and it is not uncommon for persons working in criminal justice to obtain legal training as well.

Let us quickly review the general career options one has when the law degree has been completed, still assuming that work in the justice system is the goal. State and local prosecution offices number over 8,000; these are the agencies engaged in the prosecution of alleged criminal offenders, although some also provide civil legal services to government. At the state level, these include the Office of the Attorney General, states' attorneys, district attorneys, and prosecuting attorneys. The titles of county-level prosecutors vary but include county attorney, corporation counsel, county solicitor, and district attorney to name a few. In contrast, a relatively new law-related agency is the Office of the Public Defender, the smallest of all criminal justice sectors. Like the prosecutor, these offices are supported by public funds, and their responsibility derives from the constitutional right to legal counsel.

Three-fourths of all public defender officers are administered by county government, and less than one-fourth by state government. The office of public defender is growing, and most public defenders now handle the full range of criminal cases, along with some civil areas. Here again is a fine example of a career that relates to criminal law and offenders but also services the needs of persons who seek legal assistance for housing, consumer welfare, and various domestic matters. Public defenders do not merely represent those charged with crimes.

There are about 17,000 courts, which represent the second largest sector of the justice system. Courts are units of the judicial branch of government with authorization, by statute or constitution, to decide con-

---

*Munneke, Gary A. *Opportunities in Law Careers.* Lincolnwood, IL: National Textbook Company, 1994.

troversies and disputed matters of fact brought before them. There are appellate, general, and limited levels of court jurisdiction. All of these employ judges, clerks, and private practice attorneys. Some also have court administrators, another relatively new career, to oversee and supervise the process. A typical court administrator might be employed under the general direction of the chief judge to manage all administrative functions of that court. These functions would include directing a staff responsible for the processing of traffic, civil, and criminal cases, as well as providing court security and many other nonlegal duties. Many positions exist for court administrators in the $40,000 range, and graduate training in public administration or court administration is required. Future growth is expected, due to continuing state-level court reorganization and the backlogs in courts, which result in delays and political pressures to alleviate them.

Jobs for bailiffs, court officers, and other nonlegal positions affiliated with court expansion are increasing. Both size and number of courts have increased in recent years, and that growth appears to be continuing. With it will continue the demand for maintaining order and the numerous other tasks of the bailiff and court officers. Other positions, such as law clerks, clerks of the court, legal stenographers, and legal transcribers also serve the court system in a supportive capacity.

The court system is always undergoing change in this country, and the occupational situation is changing and improving. Not only are increased personnel to be expected, but greater specialization and newly expanded duties as well.

Judges, who may serve in any number of different jurisdictional levels, basically listen to testimony, rule on what evidence may be acceptable, and either decide the case or instruct the jury on the law and their options for a decision. Numbers of judicial positions have been on the increase, again due to backlogs and increased criminal trials. There are district courts, juvenile and traffic courts, appeals courts, probate courts, municipal courts, and of course supreme courts. Nearly all judges now have legal training and extensive courtroom trial experience. Salaries will vary considerably according to the level of jurisdiction and responsibility. A salary of $90,000 would not be unusual for a state supreme court justice, and the United States Supreme Court justices currently receive a salary of $140,000. In most jurisdictions, judges are elected for specific terms, although at the federal level they are appointed for life. District level judges in the federal system are paid $95,000; U.S. Appeals Court judges receive $105,000 in salary. Salaries might be less for those in municipal, juvenile, and other local courts with a range, depending upon type of jurisdiction, of $65,000–$85,000. Pay raises in the federal system are under continuous review because of the reluctance of qualified personnel to leave private law practices. Also under review in many states are other means of selecting judges so they need not campaign and run for re-election so often.

We have described briefly the main actors in the court; other lawyers are employed by government to research and prepare legislation. The police legal advisor has already been mentioned as a newly established career for those lawyers who wish to remain, or to become affiliated, with a police agency. Many political careers and judicial careers are launched by first serving as the local prosecutor or county attorney. The lawyer, and more recently, the court administrator, are interwoven into the system, and many career opportunities are projected for this area of public service.

CORRECTIONS AND REHABILITATION

With the public expressing increased concern over violent crime and repeat offenders, sentencing trends in recent years have been toward more institutional confinement for longer periods of time. This has resulted in a virtual explosion of the inmate population in federal, state, and local correctional facilities, along with numerous employment opportunities. In fact, if current trends continue, corrections will continue to be the growth industry of the criminal justice system well into the twenty-first century.

Consider that more than 5.1 million people were under correctional supervision in the United States in the latest count. Nearly three million of these adults were under community supervision (probation) and an additional 700,000 were on parole—conditional supervised release after serving a prison term. Very soon this figure will represent nearly 3 percent of the entire U.S. adult population.

States with the largest prison populations are Texas, California, and New York, who along with Florida and the Federal Bureau of Prisons account for 40 percent of all inmates.

With one million, one hundred thousand offenders behind bars, the search for correctional officer personnel will continue at a rapid pace for some time to come, and career seekers will do well to give consideration to employment in this important human service occupation. (See chart at the end of this chapter.)

Yet, because corrections does not have as much public visibility as police or the courts, the wide array of jobs available is often overlooked. Depending upon one's personal interests, employment in corrections can be found in any number of settings: in an institutional facility as a sworn correctional officer; with a probation office supervising offenders in the community; as a caseworker whose clients require specialized attention; or as a correctional counselor dealing with the personal problems and individual circumstances of inmates, probationers, or parolees. Since institutions—from local county jails to large maximum security penitentiaries—all are communities within themselves, corrections also includes positions ranging from work supervisors to teachers, chaplains, medical personnel, psychologists, and many others, as well as the command staff, most of whom began as sworn correctional officers.

As with police departments, correctional institutions are found at all levels of government. At the local level, one might seek employment in the jail, a stockade, a women's facility, a halfway house, a regional center for youthful offenders, or a specialized facility, such as group homes dealing with addictions. Some local jail staff are employed as deputy sheriffs and cross-trained in law enforcement in order to serve as patrol deputies as well.

The Correctional Officer

As reported by the *1993 Sourcebook of Criminal Justice Statistics,* there were 600,000 persons employed in local, state, and federal correctional facilities as officers. The largest single group of employees in this system are *correctional officers.* Like their police counterparts, correctional officers are sworn employees at the entry-level of the system. Those wishing to advance to higher ranks can always expect to serve for some time as a correctional officer, since most promotions are made from within the agency.

Generally speaking, the correctional officer of today has some higher education, plus training in subjects ranging from emergency response to interpersonal communications. Especially in the case of facilities that specialize in housing and treating youthful offenders, officers may receive special training in modifying behavior.

GENERAL DUTIES

The challenge of the correctional officer is to maintain security of the institution and safety of the inmate population, while gaining the acceptance needed to assist the offender in developing socially acceptable behavior for release back into the community. As the direct supervisors of the inmates entrusted to them, correctional officers are responsible for their care, custody, and control. Correctional officers therefore enforce institutional rules and take action when violations occur. But officers also need to balance rule enforcement with empathy and consideration of the offender's needs in order to obtain the respect and trust necessary to carry out their duties effectively.

DISTINGUISHING FEATURES OF THE JOB CLASS

Work as a correctional officer involves daily interaction with inmates—from processing their entry into the institution, to supervising their activities while confined, to transporting them outside of the facility as needed, to processing their release paperwork. Although officers have access to a supervisor at all times, much of the work is performed independently, requiring considerable discretion. In any institutional setting, there is some element of danger. However, riots are rare events, and experience has shown that even when such disturbances do occur, officers who had a reputation for treating inmates firmly but fairly often were not harmed. Although weapons are not permitted inside of correctional facilities, assignments such as outside perimeter patrol and inmate transportation will require qualification with firearms.

ILLUSTRATIVE EXAMPLES OF WORK

Specific duties of correctional officers vary somewhat, depending on the type and size of the facility. In smaller institutions, officers are expected to perform a wide variety of tasks, whereas those in more specialized or larger systems may be assigned to one particular duty post. General functions include responsibility for security of the institution, control of contraband (prohibited items), and supervision of the many repair, maintenance, manufacturing, and other inmate work services—from furniture factories to farming operations. In addition significant counseling functions may be included at those institutions that are committed to the use of correctional officers in the rehabilitation process. More specific tasks include:

- Communicating with the inmates to develop effective interpersonal relations and assist their adjustment to incarceration
- Maintaining inmate order and discipline by patrolling corridors, inspecting cell blocks, and enforcing rules and regulations
- Preventing escapes through visual alertness, promptly responding to any information obtained about escape attempts, and conducting routine search procedures
- Keeping accurate inmate records upon intake, during confinement, and upon release
- Supervising recreation, work details, visiting, and all other inmate activities
- Handling inmate problems and requests for services (commissary items, medical treatment, and religious services)
- Transporting inmates to court appearances, medical offices, and other correctional facilities
- Conducting frisk, strip, and cell searches to detect contraband
- Screening visitors to ensure that they are authorized and not introducing contraband
- Conducting regular headcounts of the inmate population
- Preparing written incident reports of rule violations
- Providing first aid in emergency situations
- Handling any physical altercations with the minimum force necessary to control the situation
- Classifying inmates according to their personal characteristics and offense record in order to make proper cell assignments.

In addition to the primary responsibility of keeping offenders safely in custody, the correctional officer in recent years has come to be recognized as an important component of the treatment process. With the limited availability of formal treatment services, and in view of the close and continual contact between staff and inmates, the role of the correctional officer in promoting behavior change is evident. In recognition of this "cell block counseling" role, many agencies are providing officers with additional training in social problems, human behavior, cultural diversity, and interpersonal communication.

REQUIRED KNOWLEDGE, SKILLS, AND ABILITIES

- Excellent interpersonal communication skills
- General intelligence and emotional stability
- Good judgment
- Ability to properly exercise discretion
- Ability to deal firmly but fairly with those incarcerated
- Ability to analyze situations quickly and take proper action
- Good powers of observation and memory
- Ability to prepare factual written reports
- Knowledge of first aid methods (after training)
- Ability to speak clearly and listen effectively
- Excellent moral character
- Physical agility

PLACES OF EMPLOYMENT

Federal Level. Federal detention centers confine aliens detained for the U.S. Immigration and Naturalization Service. Approximately 24,000 staff members are employed by the Federal Bureau of Prisons in facilities throughout the country. Most of these positions are correctional services, (primarily correctional officers and treatment personnel), but opportunities also exist in related classifications such as educational programs, recreational activities, religious services, food preparation, correctional industries, mechanical maintenance, psychological and medical services, management, and administration. Working for the Federal Bureau of Prisons is working for the federal government and as a part of the U.S. Department of Justice. More than 200 separate occupational categories are encompassed within these seventy institutions nationwide.

Ever since its creation in 1930, this agency has been a leader in developing modern approaches to correctional planning and management. Its staff is well trained and committed to upholding very high standards of performance. Its operations are regionalized to expedite administration, and career opportunities are also available in the six regional offices and in the headquarters in Washington, DC.

The largest number of entry-level openings in the Federal Bureau of Prisons are for correctional officers and treatment specialists. Correctional officers at the federal level perform generally the same functions as their state and local counterparts. They are responsible for guiding inmate conduct, supervising work details, carrying out plans for inmate treatment, instructing and counseling inmates, and ensuring the custody, safety, and well-being of the inmate population. Applicants must be U.S. citizens, no more than thirty-seven years of age, in good physical condition, and subject to a security clearance. Also, applicants must demonstrate that they have had three years of relevant work experience, although completion of a four-year degree may be substituted for three years of experience. Those selected are appointed at the GS-5 level ($24,000), with potential for advancement to the next grade after six months of satisfactory service. Treatment specialists begin at the GS-6 level with a degree.

Correctional treatment specialists employed by the Federal Bureau of Prisons perform correctional casework in an institutional setting. They develop, evaluate, and analyze program needs of the inmates; assess their progress; coordinate inmate training programs; develop social histories; provide case reports to the U.S. Parole Commission; develop parole and release plans; conduct individual and group interviews; and coordinate with family members. Applicants must meet the same general requirements listed above for the position of correctional officer. In addition candidates must have a bachelor's degree with at least twenty-four semester hours of social sciences, plus two years of graduate study in social science, or two years of supervised casework experience, or a combination of both.

Regardless of their specific job classification, employees of the Federal Bureau of Prisons are first and foremost correctional workers, with specialization secondary to that primary role. Therefore, all employees participate in a core training program consisting of interpersonal communication skills, firearms, self-defense, hostage policy, report writing, legal issues, employee conduct, supervisory skills, and other fundamental topics. Refresher and specialized training are provided as needed throughout the employee's career.

As with other law enforcement and correctional agencies, the Bureau of Prisons maintains high standards of personal conduct for employees, both in the workplace and in the community. This is perhaps an even greater concern in corrections, where employees work daily with a sophisticated inmate population, many of whom actively seek to manipulate staff. Personal integrity, honesty, and good moral character are therefore essential qualifications of all correctional employees.

The Immigration and Naturalization Service, also within the U.S. Department of Justice, employs 1,100 detention and deportation officers. Their duties are specific to alien and immigrant matters whenever a federal crime is involved. In recent years their numbers have been increasing since illegal entry and forced deportation of criminal, nonviolent offenders has been getting much public and political attention.

Another group of federal officers, some 4,000 in number, are primarily responsible for probation and parole supervision of federal offenders. These officers work for the Administrative Office of the U.S. Courts. They are almost entirely assigned to Texas, California, Florida, and New York. A similar distribution would hold true for the detention and deportation officers cited above.

Benefits and job security are attractive features of federal employment, along with promotional opportunities. However, employees seeking promotion must generally be willing to transfer to other areas of the country. Those covered by the special retirement provisions for law enforcement and correctional personnel may retire at age fifty with twenty years of service, with retirement at age fifty-five available for those with 25 years of such service.

Those interested in employment with the Federal Bureau of Prisons can obtain an application by contacting the National Recruitment Office, 320 First Street, NW, Washington, DC 20534.

State and Local Levels. The state level offers the greatest number of correctional employment opportunities. More than 400,000 employees work in corrections at the state level, which represents 61 percent of the total correctional positions available in the country. Such personnel are predominately employed in the approximately 1,000 state adult confinement institutions and community-based facilities spread throughout the United States. These might include prisons, diagnostic and reception centers, drug or alcoholic treatment centers, prison farms, road camps, boot camps, and community-based settings such as halfway houses, pre-release facilities, and youthful offender institutions. Some 95 percent of inmates housed in state corrections systems are confined in prisons; only about 5 percent are within community-based settings. Employment potential in community-based correctional work varies; some states have no such program, and several states, notably Florida, Michigan, and Pennsylvania, have many. All states have at least one major prison, and highly populated states can have a dozen or more.

Listed among the 1,100 publicly operated juvenile facilities are detention centers, group homes, ranches, forestry camps, and training schools. Many are state-operated, but an equal number are county-administered. Very few are at the city level, although juvenile programs and facilities are increasingly operated by private enterprise (particularly in Florida). The largest numbers of specialized facilities for juveniles and youth are found in California, with New York and Ohio next. There has been a recent trend to increase the number of smaller, minimum security facilities in order to focus more specialized treatment and attention on persons with the best hope for rehabilitation. Juveniles with more frequent and serious arrest records were previously housed in local jails. However, courts are now requiring that juveniles be separated from adults, thus creating more separate juvenile facilities, even for the hard-core offender. Although those under eighteen are generally considered juveniles, this varies depending on the jurisdiction, the offender's prior record, and the seriousness of the offense. Overall employment potential is expected to continue to expand for those interested in working with youth, whether in security or treatment-related positions.

Among institutions housing adults, the nation's 3,200 local jails confine those waiting for trial or sentenced to a year or less, whereas state facilities house those serving sentences longer than one year. In fact almost half of jail residents are unconvicted—meaning that they have either not yet gone to trial or have not yet been arraigned. Jails also hold those awaiting either sentencing or transfer to state prison. As a result clients in the local system tend to turn over rapidly, and, therefore, less emphasis is usually placed on long-term treatment or rehabilitation. It is also interesting to note that nearly half of all jail inmates nationwide are confined in only 5 percent of the jails. For example, the Los Angeles megajail system is the largest in the free world—housing a daily population that exceeds 22,000 inmates. With thousands of staff members servicing the security and general living needs of inmates in megajail systems, it is apparent that better employment and promotional opportunities will be found among the larger jails in major metropolitan areas. However, opportunities are expanding in many smaller jurisdictions as well, and the 200,000 personnel working in local corrections represent 35 percent of the employment in corrections nationwide.

Since jails are the first point of contact for offenders, they are also the first to feel the impact of increasing crime rates. To reduce jail populations to more manageable levels, pretrial release programs and electronic monitoring are being used more often as an alternative to incarceration. These efforts involve selecting offenders whose community ties, work record, and lack of prior convictions make them good risks for appearing at trial. Many are released into the community with close supervision. Others are placed in home detention through the use of electronic surveillance that monitors their movements outside of a specified area. These new trends toward home detention and pretrial release have created additional jobs for civilians supervising the activities and reporting requirements of those released. Some pretrial release programs fall under the jurisdiction of the courts; others are the responsibility of the local jail system.

Administratively, the majority of jails are managed by a sheriff's office; however, some jails are administered at the state level. These include Connecticut, Delaware, Rhode Island, Vermont, and Hawaii. Another alternative that some jurisdictions are exploring is contracting out the operation of jails to private firms. In a few areas of the country, this new approach is becoming increasingly popular. No longer is private contracting limited to a few functions that jails are not well-equipped to handle, such as food or medical services. Throughout the country, private contracting historically has been found more often in juvenile and community-based facilities than in adult detention. But today there is a very significant movement in many states to contract the prison construction and operation to private companies. Some of these companies include Wackenhut Corrections, Corrections Corporation of America, and Esmor Correctional Services to name a few. In all cases, as the contracts increase, employment opportunities will continue to expand. Although one would technically be employed by the private corporation, there will still be job requirements as established by that state. Thus applicants will still be screened and trained according to prevailing standards.

Pretrial release, home detention, electronic surveillance, and private contracting are among the options correctional administrators have explored to cope with a continually growing inmate population. But the most frequent response by far has been construction of new jails and prisons, which is occurring at a pace unprecedented in the history of corrections. The observation that there are fewer jails now than there were several years ago, possibly a loss of some eighty per year, does not impact negatively on job opportunities. The larger regional jails, being built in such states as Virginia, West Virginia, and Kentucky, all will employ more officers and specialists than some of those smaller jails ever did. Many of these construction projects involve *new generation facilities.* As described by the National Institute of Corrections,* new generation facilities can be compared to the next generation of computers, whose capabilities improve with each new model. They are designed on the basis of state-of-the-art concepts developed by architects and psychologists about how institutions affect human behavior. New generation structures are physically constructed to increase safety and security through architectural design, while at the same time, providing more humane living conditions. In contrast to older institutions where cell bars separated officers from the inmates, officers directly supervise inmates in new generation facilities with no physical barriers between them. It is for this reason that the new generation concept is also called *direct supervision.*

---

*This discussion of new generation facilities has been summarized from NIC's publication entitled *New Generation Jails: An Innovative Approach to an Age-Old Problem* by Stephen H. Gettinger, (March, 1984; available free of cost from the National Institute of Corrections, Longmont, CO 80501).

Rather than patrolling corridors, direct supervision officers are stationed in a dormitory-style living area, where they directly control privileges, enforce rules and regulations, and closely supervise the inmate population. This is a dramatic change from traditional facility design, where an officer's ability to control inmates is more limited because there is less opportunity for contact and interaction. Largely because of their more pleasant atmosphere, new generation facilities have been found to reduce such traditional problems as tension, violence, noise, and idleness. Since inmates tend to take more pride in their living conditions, vandalism is rare, and peer pressure keeps the physical environment in good condition. There is also considerably more freedom of movement, as well as inmate access to telephones, recreation, and TV. Thus, there is a subtle pressure to conform to institutional rules and regulations in order to avoid losing these privileges.

Although officers are at first sometimes resistant to the direct inmate contact required in new generation facilities, most overcome any initial reservations after working in such a setting. When they realize that they have more authority, fewer inmate disciplinary problems, less concern for personal safety, and greater opportunities to participate in management decisions, the officers themselves often become strong advocates for the direct supervision approach. Moreover, correctional systems building new generation institutions tend to place a substantial emphasis on training officers in direct supervision techniques and interpersonal communication skills.

Although "new generation" represents the state-of-the-art in corrections, it is only in recent years that this trend has begun to influence the field. As new building projects are undertaken, there will undoubtedly be more direct supervision models. Although the vast majority of existing correctional systems reflect older designs, new generation facilities can now be found in many major metropolitan areas—New York, Buffalo, Chicago, San Diego, San Jose, Tucson, Las Vegas, Portland, Miami, Tampa, Alexandria (Virginia), Contra Costa (California), and Prince Georges County (Maryland). As in most correctional institutions—whether new generation or not—tours are available upon request. Those seeking employment in correctional facilities are therefore encouraged to contact the nearest local, state, or federal facility and arrange a tour to get a first hand view of working conditions and officer duties.

Of the approximately 200,000 local and 400,000 state correctional employees, the majority are in the classification of correctional officer. Salaries vary greatly for these sworn, uniformed officers, tending to increase with the size of the facility at the local level and to be standardized throughout the state for state employees (although cost-of-living differentials are sometimes provided in metropolitan areas). Starting levels tend to be around $20,000 for state officers. With overtime, night differential for evening shifts, and regular increases, an average correctional officer is probably earning in the $21,000 to $26,000 range. The current starting salary for state officers assigned to southeast Florida is $23,100. In some jurisdictions, collective bargaining units have successfully obtained pay parity with law enforcement officers, so salaries in heavily unionized sections of the country tend to be closer to that listed previously for police officers. In addition, large megajail systems generally compensate quite well. For example, Dade County (Miami, Florida) maintains a sworn correctional officer staff of approximately 1,600 and offers a starting salary of about $26,000 depending on shift assignment, with the potential of advancing to $29,000 to $30,000 in this entry-level rank. Among other large county jail systems, salaries are equally attractive: $32,000, Los Angeles; $30,000, San Francisco; $23,000, Seattle; $21,000 Tampa. Of course, jurisdictions with higher starting salaries are also likely to be more selective. In addition to traditional age, citizenship, and physical requirements, applicants can also be expected to be subjected to a polygraph examination, extensive background investigation, reading and writing tests, physical agility assessment, and/or psychological examination. A medical history, including drug test, can be expected as well.

Probation and Parole. Career opportunities in corrections extend beyond secure institutions. Some offenders leave the courtroom and are placed on probation, which does not entail any form of confinement. Others, released after serving part of their sentence, are on parole or some other form of supervised release.

More than 72,000 employees work in probation or parole, and they are about evenly divided between state and local jurisdictions. Salaries vary greatly for these correctional employees, nearly all of whom are college graduates. Compensation reflects the prevailing wages in the area where they are employed—which could be as modest as $25,000 for a juvenile court counselor, or as high as $40,000 for an experienced parole supervisor. Much depends upon the type of agency one is serving. Probation officers (sometimes called agents) have responsibility for compiling presentence investigations for the court. This officer may also be asked to make a formal court report and a recommendation to the judge for case disposition. In some locales there are investigators who conduct such investigations and compile information for the probation officer. Regardless of the size and volume of the jurisdiction, however, the probation officer is the professional responsible for advising and counseling the caseload of individuals placed on probation by the court. This counseling includes personal matters, social adjustment, work and economic circumstances, and all areas that would influence the required adjustment of the offender.

A recent survey of probation and parole agency directors cited increasing caseloads and workload management as by far the most critical concern. These same directors were especially concerned about the adequacy of substance abuse programs and the heavier caseloads that are due to increases in substance abuse without accompanying resources. Other special needs expressed by these probation and parole directors were the need for more intensive monitoring of clients with mental illness, more treatment capacities for sex offenders, and the importance of expanding electronic monitoring in all jurisdictions.

In addition to counseling, job placement, and traditional social work–oriented functions, probation officers must enforce the rules imposed on the client by the court. Conditions of probation could include regular school attendance, abstinence from alcohol and/or drugs, participation in treatment programs, adherence to curfew hours, refraining from criminal associations, and the like. Thus, many probation officers find their role requires a delicate balance of social worker and rule-enforcer. Some jurisdictions use teams of specialized officers, with one employee responsible for counseling, another for developing community contacts, and another for violation enforcement. But this approach is relatively unique, and it is far more common to find all of these tasks included in the combined function of each probation officer.

Probation work exists with both juveniles and adults; and in all cases a plan must be formulated for directing and enforcing an effective rehabilitation arrangement. Much of the work of a probation officer involves contact with family, employers, and others whose lives affect the person on probation. Anyone interested in probation as a career would usually possess a bachelor's degree in the social sciences, human behavior, or criminal justice. At the graduate level, a master's degree is often required for supervisory duties and promotion. That degree might be in social work, or in a field that relates closely to understanding and influencing human behavior.

Parole officers do much the same type of work, and have many of the same kinds of responsibilities. However, their clientele have already served time in institutions and have been released conditionally *on parole.* Hence, the parolee may require more intensive supervision, and in some cases, group therapy and other behavior adjustment techniques. The parole officer may have to arrange for the client to find a place to live or a job, and may also have to enforce the specific conditions of release.

There are various opportunities for advancement and career development in both probation and parole, including intensive case loads for therapy and counseling purposes, field supervisors, office managers, and district or regional administrators. These positions function at both federal and state levels, as well as local and county levels. They also service juveniles, young adults, and adult offenders. There are institutional parole officers, whose tasks involve assisting the inmate prior to early release or supervising the adjustment process for those about to be released. Although caseloads tend to be high, the work is challenging and rewarding. An excellent way to learn more about this field is to ask to perform an internship as part of the college educational experience. Many probation and parole offices welcome college students who can assist in investigations and participate in basic offender supervision work.

Additional Correctional Opportunities. Within this extensive field ranging from pretrial services to probation, custody, treatment, rehabilitation, and parole, there are many additional jobs that have not been discussed. For example, in correctional facilities, numerous employment possibilities exist beyond the correctional officer. These include the *living unit supervisor* (cottage parent), the various *industry shop supervisors,* those involved in *inmate reception and classification,* and a variety of special assignments related to counseling, treatment, record keeping, and maintenance of the institution. In the latter case, the facility may be a farm, a lumber camp, or a unit assigned to road construction and repair. In such types of correctional units, the officer often doubles as *job supervisor* and *personal counselor.*

The list of the correctional personnel categories in appendix B demonstrates the variety of job opportunities within the field. This list is an excellent indication of the number of trained staff required to effectively administer programs in criminal justice. Some serve at the beginning of the process, as in the case of gang workers in social agencies; some are employed in the pretrial phase; and others are utilized to administer the correctional system either in institutions or through such community-based processes as probation and parole.

CRIMINALISTICS AND THE CRIME LAB

The career field that is perhaps most directly related to enforcement but that occurs in the laboratory and not on the street, is called *criminalistics* or forensic science. There are several paths into this scientific area, depending on the specialty. Most frequently the criminalist is someone who majored in chemistry or physics and who has experience in applying this scientific competence to physical evidence and the questions of the criminal investigator.

The criminalist obtains experience through an internship while in college, and later, while employed in a crime laboratory. Because of the shortage of qualified persons in criminalistics, particularly those with graduate degrees, there are also opportunities to become a director of such a lab. Some criminalists prefer not to become involved in the administrative duties of a lab director, however, and therefore are employed as scientists engaged in the critical task of determining facts through their highly technical knowledge.

The *forensic scientist* is a more highly skilled and specialized scientific investigator in a single area of physical evidence analysis. As such, the forensic scientist generally is not as concerned with all physical/legal aspects of evidence as is the criminalist. The services of both are crucial to enforcement agencies, as well as to the defense. Opportunities are always available for those who prepare for such careers through a background in the natural and physical sciences.

As with general enforcement work, there are laboratories at all jurisdictional levels. Some federal agencies have extensive facilities. Most notable are those of the FBI, drug enforcement, and post office departments. All states have labs serving the headquarters of their state enforcement unit, in addition to other state labs that provide testing services primarily for the regulatory units in state government. Most major cities also have crime labs. Others, frequently known as regional forensic labs, assist local departments in their entire region, so there are a number of locations for such employment.

In addition to the work of the chemist and physicist, there are lab-staffing needs in such fields as the polygraph (lie detector), the examination of questioned documents, fingerprint identification, and ballistics (firearms and tool identification), all of which require personal experience following considerable, on-the-job training. Once the examiner qualifies as an expert, much of his or her time is spent testifying in courts. If one has a scientific and inquisitive mind, the work of the criminalist or laboratory-forensic examiner beckons.

The criminalist or forensic scientist, whether a biologist, chemist, or physicist, conducts tests related to a specialized area of science. The chemist may make determinations as to whether a stain is truly blood, whether a pill contains a narcotic drug, or whether a paint chipping came from a particular automobile fender. The physicist may make analyses of metals, glass, or other materials. Their primary concern in testing is to establish positive identifications and relationships to crimes, and their findings may determine a suspect's innocence or guilt.

There is optimism about the job market for the forensic science specialist because surveys indicate that over 500 new people are needed each year. Since there are only some twenty graduate programs nationwide in forensic sciences, there continue to be vacancies for qualified individuals; salaries range from $35,000 to $48,000 for those with scientific educational preparation and will be greater with experience and in the largest laboratories, such as the federal agency labs.

Forensic science, therefore, is a broad field in which physical and biological sciences are used to analyze and evaluate physical evidence related to law. Physical evidence is any physical item with potential for providing information to the criminal justice system, civil litigations, or other matters of public interest and concern. Besides the criminalists, the forensic pathologists, and forensic toxicologists, these sciences include document examiners, anthropologists, psychiatrists, and a variety of chemists and others. Some departments and laboratories employ technicians who are skilled in certain instrumentation, but not necessarily in all aspects of the scientific profession. In preparation, one would normally follow a course of study through chemistry, instrumental analysis and microscopy, other sciences such as biology as they relate to evidence, and selected legal courses. For technician positions, one should complete as much high school math and science as possible and then look to more basic sciences in the community college. More and more departments now employ personnel under the titles of crime scene technician, lab technician, or crime analyst. These jobs may require high school graduation and further academic study is encouraged after employment. Positions such as identification technician provide excellent experience and training on-the-job in photography, evidence collection, preparing reports and classifying fingerprints, while permitting access to higher education as well.

Let us review some of the specialized examiners and scientists who are found within the forensic laboratory.

THE POLYGRAPH OPERATOR AND THE DOCUMENT EXAMINER

The *polygraph operator,* or lie detector examiner, should have a working knowledge of human behavior and psychological responses. Through skillful testing of victims, suspects, witnesses, and others, this person is often able to determine whether or not an individual's verbal responses are truthful. The process of getting truthful responses is a delicate one, and the examiner must have a sound knowledge of both personality differences and interviewing techniques. Again, and most importantly, the polygraph operator may determine one's *lack* of involvement in a particular criminal situation.

The *document examiner* has a variety of skills and tools with which to work. This specialist may be called on to analyze the signature on a check or compare known samples of a suspect's handwriting with a ransom note. In a more mechanical way, the document examiner may be asked to find out if a particular typewriter was used in the preparation of a deceased person's final will or whether the age of the ink and the age of the paper correspond on an alleged valuable document.

Document examiners deal with questions that need not always be criminal matters. One might be asked to help resolve cases involving the ages of conflicting or contested wills. Or one might be asked to resolve questions of signature authenticity in autographs, property deeds, and ownership titles.

FINGERPRINT AND FIREARMS EXPERT

The *expert in fingerprint identification* begins to obtain experience by classifying and comparing the many fingerprints on file in both criminal and noncriminal record systems. After considerable experience in making positive identifications and testifying to these in court, an examiner may become regarded as an expert. The importance of this means of identification cannot be overstressed, since it continues to this date to be our most positive single means of providing proof of individual identity. The expert in this field also will be called upon to make determinations in the case of footprints, palm prints, and other less common but equally positive sources.

The *firearms identification expert* is most frequently portrayed firing a revolver into a container and then making microscopic comparisons of the bullet in order to discover whether or not that particular weapon fired the suspect bullet. While such activities occupy some time, this specialist also is asked questions about whether a certain piece of metal came in contact with a specific door of a safe, or if a suspected burglary tool can positively be placed at the scene of a known break-in. The expert may also determine the distance that a shot was fired, the direction from which a bullet came, and what type of weapon was presumably used in a crime. The *firearms expert* deals with more than guns; all types of weapons and instruments are tested and compared.

THE LAB TECHNICIAN

The increased demand in recent years for analysis of blood, drugs, and alcohol has highlighted the importance of a well-staffed laboratory. As has been pointed out by the Supreme Court, the police must rely more on scientifically determined physical evidence than on suspects' confessions.

In the crime laboratory, there are employment possibilities as a *laboratory technician*. Technicians' specific duties depend on the area of the lab in which they function, and it is possible, through continuing formal education and on-the-job experience to become an examiner and, ultimately, an expert in the field. Otherwise there would be little potential for advancement in this highly specialized setting.

Outside of the laboratory, careers exist in the field of physical evidence. *Evidence technicians* are primarily responsible for the collection and packaging of all physical evidence at the crime scene and are expected to be proficient in the use of photographic equipment and in making sketches and plaster casts. The evidence technician, then, is responsible for the proper identification of suspicious items at the crime scene and for their safe delivery to the laboratory examiner.

More and more, lab work is being done in mobile crime laboratories, and this will demand more field personnel to inspect crime scenes, collect items for analysis, and perform necessary tests for later court presentation.

Some evidence technicians are police officers; some are civilians. The vehicles they use are equipped with everything from illumination devices, to facilities for field analyses of various kinds. They take photographs, make plaster and plastic casts, search out fingerprints and other forms of offender traces, and operate a vacuum to collect hairs and fibers. They must be able to collect and preserve properly any significant finding.

Forensic chemists, the most common laboratory professionals, are responsible for determining any connections that exist between case evidence and suspects. They conduct microscopic examinations and chemical tests on materials such as hair, fibers, skin, paint, glass, dirt, poisons, drugs, fabrics, gases, and substances of all types. Most of these tests, known as X-ray spectrometers, chromatography, ultra-violet and infrared spectrometers, and micro-photography, analyze unknown substances to determine and identify any significance to a crime. These chemists will be called upon to ascertain if a located sample is blood and if so, what type, and any other factors that can be indicated from that sample. Other body fluids can also be evaluated for positive linkages to offenders, victims, and suspects. Many new techniques have been introduced into the modern crime lab and precision instruments such as electronic cell counters, computers, and electronic microscopes demand both formal training and experience on-the-job. For one who has persistence, and not just patience, a talent for scientific inquiry, and a determination that can overcome the unpleasant odors, sights, and other frustrations, the employment outlook is quite favorable in the forensic lab, and it is projected to continue to be so for the foreseeable future.

A specialist position not affiliated with the crime laboratory, but one with technical expertise in receiving, analyzing, and assessing criminal information is the criminal analyst. These personnel receive confidential information and analyze data, prepare reports, and disseminate information to assist in criminal investigations or intelligence assessments. Their unique type of work studies criminal groups, methods of operations, extent of criminal influences, and makes recommendations for investigative strategies.

All of the personnel in this section—as is the case with detectives and investigators—must have an ability to evaluate, analyze, and present information accurately. They must communicate clearly and have the capacity to apply logic and sound judgement to criminal operations. The ability to prepare reports and illustrative devices and to use data to one's advantage are all paramount. Computer skills, too, are essential.

PRIVATE SECURITY AND LOSS PREVENTION

Yearly crime-related losses to the business, retail, and industrial community total an estimated one hundred billion dollars a year. This figure includes employee theft and embezzlement and customer shoplifting. The market for an alternative to public policing has been growing rapidly. Over twelve million businesses and commercial establishments, from Fortune 500 companies to neighborhood markets, recognize that the half-million plus public police personnel are not sufficient to provide the necessary protection. This flourishing industry has grown at a 10 to 12 percent rate since the 1970s, and it is now a 50 billion dollar industry.

Estimates currently place the number of private security employees at 1.5 million, making them far larger than the public sector. In terms of employment, and in terms of dollar amounts actually expended on protection, the private sector is ahead. This would include contracted closed circuit and alarm monitoring services as well as more traditional armored cars and uniformed officers.

Estimates range up to 12,000 as to the number of firms and companies that provide various forms of security and protection. Many of them are one person firms owned by a former police or military officer. Since corporate America is so much more security conscious today, there will continue to be a 5 to 7 percent demand for employment within this marketplace annually.

Locations to be serviced range from colleges to hotels; from airports to museums; from subway systems to financial institutions; and the requirements and rewards are just as varied. Twenty-three states have now enacted standards and training legislation, and as these training requirements increase, so will the salaries. Presently an armed and trained private security officer can expect to earn between $1,000 and $1,500 per month. A medium-sized organization will pay $45,000 to $50,000 for its director of security. The national average for all private security directors today is $45,000. Highest director salaries are in utilities and manufacturing companies.

Recent studies indicate that well over 1.5 million persons are employed within the framework of private industrial and retail security work. This can range from traditional *guards,* who are responsible for security in buildings and grounds, to *bank guards* and *railroad police* and can extend into sophisticated assignments, such as *insurance investigation and loss prevention specialists.* Private security expenditures emphasize crime prevention through locks, alarms, patrol, TV surveillance, and other means of guarding persons and property.

In addition to the private security efforts of industry and business, there are numerous such employees who are assigned to specialized duties, but are on a public government payroll. This might include airport security personnel, college and university safety and security departments, the subway, tunnel, and harbor police. The 1977 Task Force Report on Private Security stated that the private security system, with over one million workers, sophisticated alarm systems and perimeter safeguards, armored trucks, advanced minicomputers, and thousands of highly skilled crime prevention experts, offers a potential for coping with crime that cannot be equalled by any other remedy or approach. Companies with the largest shares of the market and a history of solid performance include CPP/Pinkerton; Burns International Security Services; Wackenhut; Wells Fargo; and American and Protective Services. Pinkerton and American are both based in California, and Wackenhut in Florida. Brinks Incorporated, best known for its armored car service, also has home security services and twenty-four-hour alarm monitoring.

Pinkerton's, which originally was founded by Allan Pinkerton, earned its reputation in the Old West. It is now a major firm with a workforce of 50,000 and revenues of 800 million dollars. These firms are well known to nearly everyone because of their uniformed guards and notices on display in stores and on doors and windows. They also become known through general company protection signs, armored trucks, residential security, and private contract investigations. Salaries and advancement potential vary greatly in such work, and an applicant would be well advised to first inquire as to the firm's reputation, since most states do have requirements set for obtaining private licenses.

Some major corporations and businesses employ their own *security forces.* Employment therein usually is attractive and stable since such persons enjoy the benefits that accompany work in private industry. As concern over internal security, employee thefts, and inventory controls becomes more widespread, many companies are developing high-level, sophisticated, security units to provide safety and security within their own facilities.

Like public peace officers, these employees may be provided with some enforcement powers and may possess communication equipment and weapons. Standards for such jobs are being raised, and the federal government has been encouraging the states to initiate minimum standards for entrance into retail and industrial security work. Guardsmark, based in Tennessee and one of the largest security firms, enjoys a reputation for high-quality personnel and stringent requirements for employment.

As one might expect in the private sector, jobs at the top are competitive and well-rewarded. The proper combination of enforcement and investigative experience, coupled with higher education and some amount of management drive and skill, can lead to a well-salaried position. Numerous former police chiefs from major cities serve as vice presidents for security and loss prevention with large corporations in the United States, and their salaries exceed those earned while they were municipal police chiefs.

Private security forces now also have major responsibilities for safety and protection of many hospitals, schools, recreation facilities, public utilities, hotels, and financial institutions. The largest of these tend to be the manufacturing and retailing fields; health care and financial institutions are close behind. One firm has a contract to provide security for U.S. embassies abroad.

Another large and growing employer is the shopping mall where numbers of stores and businesses join together to purchase the contract services of a security firm, or perhaps, actually employ the officers themselves.

Private sector security firms, such as Wackenhut, are moving into the prison business, too. A potential growth area will be the operating of detention and short-term lock-up facilities. Thus, along with protecting nuclear sites, power plants, embassies in foreign lands, and many global airports, there now is the business of constructing and operating jail and detention centers. A firm such as Wackenhut provides a most modern career opportunity by combining sophisticated training and protection duties at a nuclear reactor site, or at utility-owned nuclear power plants. Such work goes a long way to dispel the image of private security employment as mere guard duty at minimum wage!

Department of Labor statistics for 1990 show that over 30 percent of new employees in security-related fields are females. The private sector has a history of employing women in security work that predates by half a century that of the public police, since it was Allan Pinkerton who hired them as early as the 1850s.

It can be expected that private sector security will continue to increase and expand, to strengthen its standards, and increase its educational requirements. As computer theft becomes more common, there will be even greater efforts to counter such crime and to employ persons with unique sets of skills. The future in this area is excellent, and one way to start is to obtain a uniformed officer security job during college. Working part-time, on varied shifts, even for minimum wage, is a way to obtain the necessary experience and reputation for dependability and resourcefulness. Some colleges even have such employment available to students studying in criminal justice.

The stigma that has long plagued this industry is that security personnel were ill-trained and low paid. As the states enact selection and training requirements, the standards are rising; and background reviews, similar to those for public police, have become the law. Florida has passed a law requiring applicants for licenses to complete twenty-four hours of training, plus twenty-eight hours for those seeking jobs that require carrying weapons.

The major firms can expect to employ personnel with police or military backgrounds, and the pay is likewise higher. These firms will provide more training than the law may require. The large firms also utilize a selective screening process that can include psychological, polygraph, and drug examinations. A wise decision in seeking such job employment or career opportunities will rest on the inquiries one makes. Thus, the state agency that licenses or regulates private security firms may be the place to start. College programs with security courses and police training centers are also sources of reliable information.

SUPPORTIVE JOBS

In addition to the aforementioned related careers, there are numerous other opportunities for employment within enforcement agencies that can be referred to as supportive. In many departments, particularly the smaller ones, some of these may be performed by sworn personnel, but more and more, especially in large cities, they have become the responsibility of civilian personnel. Some of these services are related to *communications,* such as receiving incoming telephone calls, dispatching officers upon request, and obtaining complaints directly from citizens. Everyone is familiar with the critical role played by the 911 operator. Others relate to the immense *record-keeping* task, and included here are services related to accident reports, fingerprint classifications, criminal history files, and routine processing of reports and case files.

Another major responsibility of any police agency is the *maintenance* of all property, and many hours are devoted to such items as evidence, lost and found items, property owned by prisoners, and impounded automobiles. Many departments employ *data analysts* who follow up on all reports submitted by officers and ensure their accuracy and proper completion. More recently, this function has involved dealing with computers and providing statistical data. Such persons may also be termed crime analysts.

Civilians also may be involved in *public information, equipment maintenance, staff training, community relations, photography, classification* and *counseling* in detention facilities, and such highly responsible duties as *comprehensive planning* and *computer analysis of crime data.* These jobs have been the result of the 1970s federal government initiatives in assisting local agencies by providing support for innovative and successful projects. A newly established career field, for example, is that of the planner in many agencies. Likewise, researchers and analysts will continue to be needed to assist with long-range forecasting of needs and directions and to assist decision makers through evaluation.

In addition there are the roles of community service officers, public service aides, and other nonsworn personnel. These positions, often involving taking complaints and reporting traffic problems and accidents, often appeal to persons who aspire to work in police departments but not as sworn officers. Of course it is not uncommon for some public service officers to choose law enforcement as a career, particularly after they have pursued part or all of a college education.

Civilian positions may appeal to the young person interested in employment within the criminal justice system who is unable to meet stringent physical or other qualifications for patrol duty. Or they may appeal to students who majored in business, economics, planning, computer science, physical sciences, information systems, or other disciplines that relate to the justice and safety systems. Civilian assignments also may be provided to former officers who are injured.

SUMMARY

A career in law enforcement is one of the most challenging in our complex society, and the demands made upon the law enforcement officer are so great that only those with excellent qualifications—physical, mental, and emotional—are selected. There is continuing community concern over the police today. The role of the police has changed in the eyes of the average citizen, and their peace-keeping and service functions have become more apparent.

As the President's Crime Commission stated in the *Task Force Report (on the) Police* in 1967:

> The demands upon police are likely to increase in number and complexity in the years ahead, and dealing adequately with current law enforcement needs requires a clear acknowledgement that police are one of the most important governmental administrative agencies in evidence today.

Not only are the police an essential governmental agency, the makeup of enforcement personnel is even more important. As the National Advisory Commission on Criminal Justice Standards and Goals noted in 1973 regarding the needs of police personnel:

> The police service must recruit and employ the caliber of personnel that are now found within our colleges and universities, those possessing intellectual curiosity, analytical ability, articulateness, and a capacity to relate the events of the day to the social, political, and historical context in which they occur.

Young persons with an interest in working with people and in contributing their talents to improving our society will certainly find a career in law enforcement appropriate and satisfying. With the new era of the computer, greater tactical flexibility, and a variety of new skills and techniques, modern peace officers are quite a contrast to predecessors on the frontier. Police are still on the firing line, but now they are armed with greater knowledge and more supporting resources than ever before. To most citizens, police are the only contact with their government and its laws. Nothing can be more rewarding than to be instantly recognized by young and old alike as the guardian of peace, order, and justice.

In conclusion, a career in law enforcement can provide a rewarding opportunity for young men and women who believe that they would like to be in the most stimulating and unpredictable of the human service occupations. As in all other human services, the greatest rewards come in the form of personal satisfaction. No career can be more important to a democracy than one that protects all citizens and is the recognized symbol of justice under our laws. But law enforcement is by no means an easy career; it is constantly changing to meet the new demands of a changing society. Today's peace officer faces challenges that cannot always be understood and/or resolved. Many of these issues reach beyond the crime problem, yet they must be met immediately. If you believe you have the personal qualifications to perform effectively in a position of tremendous responsibility, you may want to consider a career in law enforcement or in one of the many related fields.

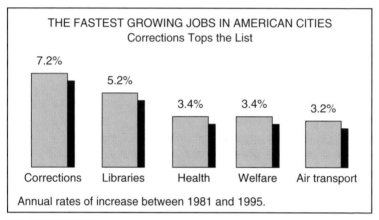

Source: U.S. Census Bureau

Percent Changes in the Number of Criminal Justice Employees, 1979–1990.

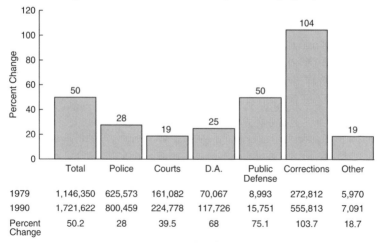

	Total	Police	Courts	D.A.	Public Defense	Corrections	Other
1979	1,146,350	625,573	161,082	70,067	8,993	272,812	5,970
1990	1,721,622	800,459	224,778	117,726	15,751	555,813	7,091
Percent Change	50.2	28	39.5	68	75.1	103.7	18.7

Source: U.S. Department of Justice, Bureau of Justice Statistics Bulletin, *Justice Expenditure and Employment, 1990* (Washington, DC: U.S. Government Printing Office, September 1992).

CHAPTER 8

NATIONAL ASSOCIATIONS

There are a number of national organizations that provide information and materials to persons interested in justice-related careers. There are also a number of federal agencies that provide career information directly and whose service also includes publications and informational handouts.

Some of the national associations and organizations are listed below:

International Association of Chiefs of Police
515 North Washington Street
Alexandria, VA 22314-2357

This large membership organization provides training courses, written materials, and a variety of other services to its members and others. The Education and Training Committee links the IACP with colleges, training academies, and the resources being produced by commercial firms.

Academy of Criminal Justice Sciences: Secretariat
Northern Kentucky University
402 Nunn Hall, Nunn Drive
Highland Heights, KY 41099-5998

Established in 1963 as the International Association of Police Professors, the Academy has broadened its base and changed its name. It is designed to further communication and research among academic personnel concerned with the many issues involved in the criminal justice professions and their relationship with higher education. Student memberships are encouraged.

National Council on Crime & Delinquency
1325 G Street NW
Suite 770
Washington, DC 20005

NCCD is a nonprofit citizen organization supported by contributions and foundations. It works to improve the criminal justice system and to maximize the effectiveness of all agencies within that system. It is especially concerned with stimulating community programs for the prevention, treatment, and control of delinquency and crime.

National Sheriffs' Association
1450 Duke Street
Alexandria, VA 22314-3490

NSA is a membership organization dedicated to furthering the goals of the Office of the Sheriff and the professional services that they represent. Career information may be available, as well as historical insights and current descriptive articles.

Lambda Alpha Epsilon
American Criminal Justice Association

Student/alumni organization with a timely and informative journal. Information about the organization and its purpose may be obtained from:

Virginia Commonwealth University
Administration of Justice & Public Safety Department
901 West Franklin Street
Richmond, VA 23284
Attn: Journal Editor, James E. Hooker

This membership fraternity, formed in San Jose, California, in 1937, welcomes preservice students as well as those already employed in the justice field. Chapters are located across the country in colleges with active criminal justice education programs.

The national office, for membership inquiries, is Post Office Box 61047; Sacramento, CA 95860.

American Jail Association
2053 Day Road, Suite 100
Hagerstown, MD 27140-9795

National Institute of Justice
National Criminal Justice Reference Service
U.S. Department of Justice
Washington, DC 20531

For reference material and resources.

Others include:

International Association of Women Police
RR 2 P.O. Box 30
Elkhart, IA 50073

American Correctional Association
    4380 Forbes Blvd.
    Lanham, MD 20706-4322

American Society of Criminology
    Ohio State University Research
    1314 Kinnear Road, Suite 212
    Columbus, OH 43212

American Society for Industrial Security
    1655 North Ft. Myer Drive, Suite 1200
    Arlington, VA 22209

Fraternal Order of Police
    1410 Donelson Pike, #A17
    Nashville, TN 37217

Additionally, each state has its own chiefs of police association, sheriff's association, and local chapters of the American Society for Industrial Security. There are also state chapters that are affiliates of the American Correctional Association in many states. All such organizations provide employment assistance or career guidance if at all possible; some maintain a permanent staff for such services.

In addition to the Federal Office of Personnel Management, there are regional federal job information/testing offices in most states, and in most major cities. Some states such as California, New York, Pennsylvania, and Texas have several locations. Contact these regional offices for job specific information, forms, and testing requirements.

Police Executive Research Forum
    1120 Connecticut Avenue NW, Suite 930
    Washington, DC 20036

Office of Fire Prevention & Arson Control
    National Emergency Training Center
    16825 South Seton Avenue
    Emmitsburg, MD 21727

National League of Cities
    1301 Pennsylvania Avenue NW
    Washington, DC 20004

Office of International Criminal Justice
    University of Illinois
    1333 South Wabash Avenue
    Chicago, IL 60605

APPENDIX A

RECOMMENDED READINGS

JOURNALS

Alpha Phi Sigma Newsletter—Alpha Phi Sigma Law Enforcement Fraternity, c/o Texas Women's University, P.O. Box 23974—TWU Station, Denton, TX 76204

American Jails—2053 Day Road, Suite 100, Hagerstown, MD 21740-9795

Corrections Today—American Correctional Association, 4380 Forbes Boulevard, Lanham, MD 20706-4322

Crime & Delinquency—National Council on Crime & Delinquency, Sage Publications, Inc., 2111 West Hillcrest Drive, Newbury Park, CA 91320

Criminal Justice International—Office of International Criminal Justice, University of Illinois at Chicago, 715 South Wood, Chicago, IL 60612

Criminology—American Society of Criminology, 1314 Kinnear Road, Suite 212, Columbus, OH 43212

FBI Law Enforcement Bulletin—FBI, U.S. Department of Justice, Washington, DC 20535

Federal Employees Almanac, Federal Employees News Digest, Inc., P.O. Box 98123, Washington, DC 20077-7263

International Criminal Police Review—ICPO—Interpol, 26 Rue Armengaud, 92210 Saint Cloud, France

Journal of Criminal Justice—Pergamon Press, Fairview Park, Elmsford, NY 10523

Journal of Forensic Sciences—American Academy of Forensic Sciences, 225 South Academy Boulevard, Colorado Springs, CO 80910

Journal of Police Science & Administration—IACP, 515 North Washington Street, Alexandria, VA 22314-2357

Journal of Security Administration—Academy of Security Educators & Trainers, 30 Falcon Drive, Hauppauge, NY 11788

Law and Order—Hendon, Inc., 1000 Skokie Boulevard, Wilmette, IL 60091

National Sheriff—1400 Duke Street, Alexandria, VA 22314

Police Chief—International Association of Chiefs of Police, 515 North Washington Street, Alexandria, VA 22314-2357

Police Studies—444 West 56th Street, New York, NY 10019

Security Management—American Society for Industrial Security, 1655 North Fort Myer Drive, Suite 1200, Arlington, VA 22209

Security World—Cahners Publishing Co., P.O. Box 5510, Denver, CO 80217

BOOKS

Abadinsky, H. *Probation & Parole,* Prentice Hall, Englewood Cliffs, NJ, 1994.

Abadinsky H. and Winfree, L. T. *Criminal Justice, An Introduction,* Nelson Hall Publishers, Chicago IL, 1994.

Adams, Thomas F. *Police Field Operations,* second edition, Prentice Hall, Englewood Cliffs, NJ, 1990.

Albanese, Jay and Pursley, Robert. *Crime in America,* Prentice Hall, Englewood Cliffs, NJ, 1993.

Allen, Harry and Simonsen C. E. *Corrections in America,* seventh edition, Prentice Hall, Englewood Cliffs, NJ, 1993.

Barker, T. Hunter, R., & Rush, J. *Police Systems and Practices,* Prentice Hall, Englewood Cliffs, NJ, 1994.

Bouza, Anthony V. *The Police Mystique,* Plenum Press, New York, NY, 1990.

Brooks, Pierce. *Officer Down: Code Three,* MTI Teleprograms, Inc., Northbrook, IL, 1975.

Chamelin & Evans. *Criminal Law for Police Officers, 5th edition,* Prentice Hall, Englewood Cliffs, NJ, 1994.

Fox, V. & Stinchcomb, J. *Introduction to Corrections, 4th edition,* Prentice Hall, Englewood Cliffs, NJ, 1994.

Inciardi, James. *Criminal Justice,* fourth edition, Harcourt, Brace Jovanovich, New York, NY, 1993.

Martin, Susan E. *Status of Women in Policing,* Police Foundation, Washington, DC, 1990.

McDowell, Charles P. *Criminal Justice in the Community,* Anderson Publishing Co., Cincinnati, OH, 1993.

Murphy, Patrick V. *Commissioner,* Simon & Schuster, New York, NY, 1977.

Niederhoffer, A. *The Police Family,* Lexington Books. D.C. Heath & Co., Boston, MA, 1978.

Ricks, T.A., Tillett, B.G. & VanMeter, C.W. *Principles of Security,* third edition, Anderson Publishing Co., Cincinnati, OH, 1994.

Schmalleger, Frank. *Criminal Justice Today,* second edition, Prentice Hall, Englewood Cliffs, NJ, 1993.

Senna, J. & Siegal, L. *Essentials of Criminal Justice,* West Publishing Co., St. Paul, Minnesota, 1995.

Sheehan, R. & Cordner, G. *Introduction to Police Administration,* third edition, Anderson Publishing Co., Cincinnati, OH, 1994.

Shusta, et al. *Multicultural Law Enforcement,* Prentice Hall, Englewood Cliffs, NJ, 1995.

Weston, P. & Wells, K. *Criminal Investigation,* sixth edition, Prentice Hall, Englewood Cliffs, NJ, 1994.

Williamson, Harold E. *The Corrections Profession,* SAGE Publications, NewBury Park, CA, 1990.

Wrobleski, H. & Hess, K. *Introduction to Law Enforcement & Criminal Justice,* third edition, West Publishing Co., St. Paul, MN, 1990.

JOB CATEGORIES IN CORRECTIONS

JOB CATEGORIES IN INSTITUTIONS

Administrators

Warden and Superintendent
Assistant/Associate Warden and
 Superintendent
Business Manager
Education Department Head
Line Correctional Staff Department
 Head
Director of Inmate Classification
Farm and Food Services Department
 Head

Maintenance Department Head
Prison Industries Superintendent
Director of Clinical/Treatment
 Services
Child Care Staff Department Head
Psychologist
Physical Education Teacher
Counselor
Institution Parole Officer
Supervisors

Line Workers

Cottage Parent/Counselor
Group Supervisor
Correctional Officers
Child Care Staff

Food and Farm Services
Maintenance
Prison Industries

JOB CATEGORIES IN PROBATION AND PAROLE AGENCIES

Administrators

Director of Court Services
Chief Probation Officer/Director
Director of Parole Supervision

Assistant/Associate Chief Probation
 Officer/Director
District Director

Supervisors

Education Supervisor
Line Correctional Staff Supervisor
Prison Industries Shop and Factory
   Head

Child Care Staff Supervisor
Supervisor of Casework Services

Functional Specialists

Academic Teacher
Vocational Teacher or Instructor
Vocational and Educational Counselor
Classification Officer

Social Worker
Sociologist
Vocational Rehabilitation Counselor

Supervisors

Staff Supervisor
District Supervisor

Assistant Supervisor
Sergeants/Lieutenants

Functional Specialists

Field Probation Officer
Psychologist

Job Placement Officer
Field Parole Officer

OTHER CORRECTIONS PERSONNEL

Chaplain
Attorney
Librarian
Medical and Dental Personnel
Training Personnel
Research Personnel

Parole Board
Parole/Probation Aide
Business and Personnel Technical
   Assistant
Others as defined by the institution or
   agency

FEDERAL BUREAU OF PRISONS

Key:
FCC—Federal Correctional Complex
FCI—Federal Correctional Institution
FDC—Federal Detention Center
FMC—Federal Medical Center
FPC—Federal Prison Camp
MCC—Metropolitan Correctional
Center

MDC—Metropolitan Detention Center
USMCFP—U.S. Medical Center for
Federal Prisoners
USP—United States Penitentiary
LSCI—Low Security Correctional Institution

MID-ATLANTIC REGION

Regional Office
10010 Junction Drive, Suite 100
North
Annapolis Junction, MD 20701

FCI Alderson, WV 24910
FCI Ashland, KY 41101
FCI Butner, NC 27509
FCI Estill, SC 29918

FCI Lexington, KY 40511
FCI Manchester, KY 40962
FCI Milan, MI 48160
FCI Morgantown, WV 26505
FCI Petersburg, VA 23804
FPC Seymour Johnson, NC 27533
USP Terre Haute, IN 47808

NORTH CENTRAL REGION

Regional Office
Gateway Complex, Inc.
Fourth and State Avenue
Kansas City, KS 66101

MCC Chicago, IL 60605
FPC Duluth, MN 55814
FCI Englewood, CO 80123
FCC Florence, CO 81292

FCC Florence, CO 81290
USP Leavenworth, KS 66048
USP Marion, IL 62959
FCI Oxford, WI 53952
FMC Rochester, MN 55903
FCI Sandstone, MN 55072
USMCFP Springfield, MO 65808
FPC Yankton, SD 57078

NORTHEAST REGION

Regional Office
U.S. Customs House, 7th Floor
Second and Chestnut Streets
Philadelphia, PA 19106

FPC Allenwood, Montgomery, PA
17752
LSCI Allenwood, White Deer, PA
17887
USP Allenwood, Watsontown, PA
17777

FCI Danbury, CT 06811
FCI Fairton, NJ 08320
FCI Fort Dix, NJ 08640
USP Lewisburg, Lewisburg, PA
17837
FCI Loretto, PA 15940
FCI McKean, Bradford, PA 16701
FCI Schuylkill, Minersville, PA 17954
MCC New York, NY 10007
FCI Otisville, NY 10963
FCI Ray Brook, NY 12977

SOUTH CENTRAL REGION

Regional Office
4211 Cedar Springs Road, Suite
300
Dallas TX 75129

FCI Bastrop, TX 78602
FCI Big Spring, TX 79720
FPC Bryan, TX 77803
FMC Carville, LA 70721
FCI El Reno, OK 73036

FPC El Paso, TX 79902
FCI Fort Worth, TX 76119
FCI LaTuna, Anthony, NM/TX 88021
FCI Memphis, TN 38134
FPC Millington, TN 38053
FCI Oakdale I, LA 71463
FCI Oakdale II, LA 71463
FCI Seagoville, TX 75159
FCI Texarkana, TX 75501
FCI Three Rivers, TX 78071

SOUTHEAST REGION

Regional Office
523 McDonough Boulevard, S.E.
Atlanta, GA 30315

USP Atlanta, GA 30315
FPC Eglin (AFB), FL 32542
MDC Guaynabo, PR 00934
FCI Jesup, GA 31545

FCI Marianna, FL 32446
MCC Miami, FL 33177
FPC Maxwell, Montgomery, AL
36112
FPC Pensacola, FL 32509
FCI Talladega, AL 35160
FCI Tallahassee, FL 32301

WESTERN REGION

Regional Office
7950 Dublin Boulevard, 3rd Floor
Dublin, CA 94002

FPC Boron, CA 93516
USP Lompoc, CA 93436
FCI Lompoc, CA 93435
MDC Los Angeles, CA 90053

FPC Nellis, NV 89191
FCI Phoenix, AZ 85027
FCI Pleasanton, Dublin, CA 94568
FCI Safford, AZ 85546
MCC San Diego, CA 92101
FCI Sheridan, OR 97378
FCI Terminal Island, CA 90731
FCI Tucson, AZ 85706

CENTRAL OFFICE

National Recruitment Office
320 First Street NW, Room 460
Washington, DC 20534

Medical Recruitment
320 First Street, NW, Room 1034
Washington, DC 20534

Staffing Office
320 First Street, NW, Room 400
Washington, DC 20534

FBOP-Examining Section (for
Correctional Officers *only*)
10010 Junction Drive, Suite 217
South
Annapolis Junction, MD 20701

FBOP-Examining Section
320 First Street, NW, Room 460
Washington, DC 20534
(for Psychologists, Medical
Officers, Physician Assistants,
Correctional Treatment and Drug
Treatment Specialists *only*)

OPPORTUNITIES IN

Accounting
Acting
Advertising
Aerospace
Agriculture
Airline
Animal & Pet Care
Architecture
Automotive Service
Banking
Beauty Culture
Biological Science
Biotechnology
Broadcasting
Building Construction Trades
Business Communications
Business Management
Cable Television
CAD/CAM
Carpentry
Chemistry
Child Care
Chiropractic
Civil Engineering
Cleaning Service
Commercial Art & Graphic
  Design
Computer Maintenance
Computer Science
Computer Systems
Counseling & Development
Crafts
Culinary
Customer Service
Data & Word Processing
Dental Care
Desktop Publishing
Direct Marketing
Drafting
Electrical Trades
Electronics
Energy
Engineering
Engineering Technology
Environmental
Eye Care
Farming and Agriculture
Fashion
Fast Food
Federal Government
Film
Financial

Food Service
Foreign Language
Forestry
Franchising
Gerontology & Aging Services
Health & Medical
Heating, Ventilation, Air
  Conditioning, and
  Refrigeration
High Tech
Home Economics
Homecare Services
Horticulture
Hospital Administration
Hotel & Motel
Human Resources
  Management
Information Systems
Installation & Repair
Insurance
Interior Design & Decorating
International Business
Journalism
Laser Technology
Law
Law Enforcement &
  Criminal Justice
Library & Information
  Science
Machine Trades
Marine & Maritime
Marketing
Masonry
Medical Imaging
Medical Technology
Mental Health
Metalworking
Military
Modeling
Music
Nonprofit Organizations
Nursing
Nutrition
Occupational Therapy
Office Occupations
Optometry
Paralegal
Paramedical
Part-Time & Summer Jobs
Performing Arts
Petroleum

armacy
otography
Physical Therapy
Physician
Physician Assistant
Plastics
Plumbing & Pipe Fitting
Postal Service
Printing
Property Management
Psychology
Public Health
Public Relations
Publishing
Purchasing
Real Estate
Recreation & Leisure
Religious Service
Restaurant
Retailing
Robotics
Sales
Science Technician
Secretarial
Social Science
Social Work
Special Education
Speech-Language Pathology
Sports & Athletics
Sports Medicine
State & Local Government
Teaching
Teaching English to Speakers
  of Other Languages
Technical Writing &
  Communications
Telecommunications
Telemarketing
Television & Video
Theatrical Design &
  Production
Tool & Die
Transportation
Travel
Trucking
Veterinary Medicine
Visual Arts
Vocational & Technical
Warehousing
Waste Management
Welding
Writing
Your Own Service Business

VGM Career Horizons
a division of *NTC Publishing Group*
4255 West Touhy Avenue
Lincolnwood, Illinois 60646-1975